LEAF AND TREE ALMANAC by Tom Frost

Commissioned by Common Ground for *LEAF!* newspaper, published by Common Ground and the Woodland Trust in the Autumn 2017 ISSUE.

LIVING WITH TREES

Grow, protect and celebrate the
trees and woods in your community

ROBIN WALTER

LITTLE TOLLER BOOKS *for*
COMMON GROUND

Published by Little Toller Books in 2020
FORD, PINEAPPLE LANE, BRIDPORT, DORSET

Living with Trees © Common Ground 2020

Foreword © Dame Judi Dench 2020

Introduction © Richard Mabey 2020

The right of Common Ground to be identified as the copyright-holder of this work has been
asserted in accordance with Copyright, Design and Patents Act 1988

Jacket photography © Graham Shackleton 2020

All illustrations and photographs © Common Ground or Robin Walter 2020 unless
otherwise stated in caption

All illustrations from *LEAF!* newspaper published by Common Ground and the
Woodland Trust © the artists

Timeline illustrations and font © Alice Patullo 2020

We have made every effort to trace the copyright-holders; in any inadvertent omission or
error please notify Little Toller Books

Printed in Great Britain by Bell and Bain Ltd, Glasgow

All papers used by Little Toller Books are natural, recyclable products made from wood
grown in sustainable, well-managed forests

A catalogue record for this book is available from the British Library

ISBN 978-1-908213-73-0

FSC
MIX
Paper from
responsible sources
FSC® C007785
www.fsc.org

PUBLISHED WITH THE SUPPORT OF:

Martin Stanley, the Woodland Trust, Trees For Cities, Habitat Aid,
Virginia Tym, Nick Mann, Sue Clifford, Angela King, Johnny Rath,
Clare M. Ferguson, Jayne Burchell, David John Simmonds, Darryl Parkin,
Julith Jedamus, Edward Hibbert, John Lord, Sarah Havens, Cathy and Fraser
Wilson, David John Simmonds, Pamela Best, Kidman Cox, Monica Lesny,
Catherine Lloyd, Shannon Smith, Richard Bradford and the many other kind
folk who donated to our crowd-funding campaign.

COMMON GROUND

Contents

21 OCTOBER 1990: APPLE DAY LAUNCHED BY COMMON GROUND IN LONDON

Common Ground's aspiration for Apple Day was to create a calendar custom, an autumn holiday, celebrating the relationship between trees and people. It was also a demonstration of the variety we are losing, not just in the orchard, but also in our landscapes, flora and fauna, and in our culture. The first Apple Day celebrations, in the old Apple Market in London's Covent Garden, brought fruit to the market after 16 years of absence. Fruit-growers and nurseries producing and selling a variety of apples and trees rubbed shoulders with juice- and cider-makers, as well as writers and illustrators with their apple books. Today, Apple Day is celebrated throughout the UK – not yet an official public holiday, but still a strong expression of community identity and the strong interconnections between people, place and nature.

Foreword

DAME JUDI DENCH

Ever since I was young, I have had a passion for trees. I adore them! The trees in my life are much-loved friends and I think of them as my extended family. I am not alone in feeling this strong connection to trees. There are millions of us around in the British Isles and many more millions around the world: tree lovers and tree-huggers, forest dreamers and twenty-first-century woodlanders. And all of us share in this passion because we are in awe of the wonderful gifts trees give: sustenance, food, shelter, medicine, inspiration and, of course, the air we breathe.

Our history is rich with trees, woods and green men, from the Green Knight and Robin Hood to Constable and Elgar. Trees are part of our past and our future, yet we can so easily take them for granted and forget to care.

We urgently need to find new ways of living with trees. We need more trees to lock up carbon, shade our towns and cities, and bring shelter and beauty to places. Trees and woods offer us wonderful opportunities for rebuilding our wider relationship with nature and will be essential in helping the next generation cope with climate change.

For over thirty years, Common Ground have worked to celebrate our longer relationship with trees and to nurture love and care for trees and woods amongst communities all over the UK. In 1990, Common Ground started Apple Day to celebrate the diversity of our landscapes and ecology, as well as the richness of our culture. They campaigned to save orchards from becoming building plots and encouraged the national spread of Community Orchards around the country. *Living with Trees*, the beautiful book you are holding, builds on this approach and brings together a cornucopia of good ideas that show us the many clever, wonderful and innovative ways in which our fellow tree lovers are bringing trees and woods closer to the heart of our communities and daily lives.

From my earliest passion for trees came my wish to do everything that I can to protect them, and make sure that they continue to be essential to our lives. Celebration is such an important part of protecting the things we love: in order to protect something I've long believed that first we must know it is there and love that it is there. Celebration reminds us how lucky we are to have such wonderful leafy neighbours, growing in our gardens, ancient woods and community orchards, reaching for the skies above playgrounds, parks and city streets.

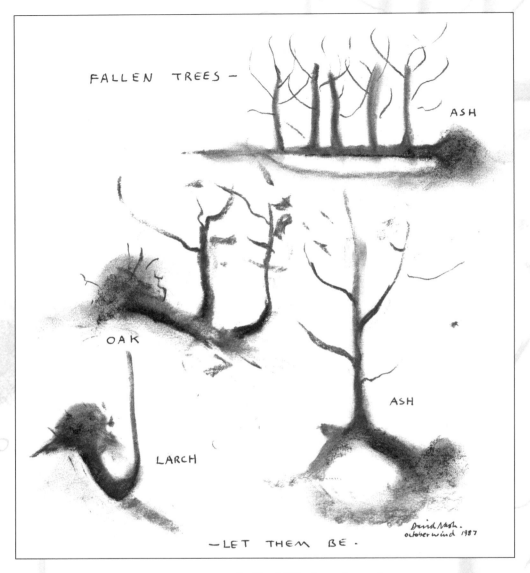

FALLEN TREES —

ASH

OAK

ASH

LARCH

— LET THEM BE .

David Nash.
october wind 1987

A FALLEN TREE IS NOT A DEAD TREE by David Nash, 1987–1989

The Great Storm of 15–16 October 1987 transformed the landscape and lives of many, unleashing a great swell of public affection for trees and woods but also a sense that an entirely natural disaster was only reparable by human intervention, by tidying, by chainsawing, clearing away the tilted or fallen trees, even if they were still alive and growing. On the morning after the storm, Common Ground turned to the artist David Nash and asked him to work on several charcoal drawings that could be printed as postcards – 56,000 of them were eventually distributed within a month of the storm, all with a simple message: a fallen tree is not a dead tree. This collaboration with Nash continued when he created the artwork for *In a Nutshell*, Common Ground's 1989 'manifesto for trees'.

#Treestoo

RICHARD MABEY

Back in those far-off days when kids were allowed to go feral in their own time, I would spend whole afternoons up a Cedar of Lebanon. Its lower storeys were like the inside of a barn, or some arboreal cave, a labyrinth of aerial passageways and cobwebbed alcoves. Our neighbourhood gang had a wealth of woody retreats in the abandoned landscape park at the back of our road, an English savanna evolving into a wilderness. There were trees for hiding in, or carving your name on, or simply gazing at. I'd often stand at the foot of a gigantic plane just for the delicious dizziness that came from staring up through the airy latticework of its branches. It had a looseness, a fluency that I found intoxicating. We built dens up birch trees and in the ginger-perfumed root-hole of a big sweet chestnut torn up in a gale. We hawked fallen walnuts to commuters taking a shortcut home across the park. Childings that we were we never gave a thought to the kind of relationship we had with the trees. It was certainly not sentimental, nor the least bit 'magical'. I think we regarded them as our companions, our co-conspirators, our context. When we exploited them, as we often did, it felt the same kind of transaction as nicking sweets from a friend. The cedars were always at the centre of it, immense evergreen pagodas, centuries old, scattered about the grassland. Our street was named after them. I lived in a cedar tree in Cedar Road.

Then one morning, a few years later, I woke to the unfamiliar sound of chainsaws. They were felling one of the trees a few hundred yards from my bedroom. It was apparently proving an inconvenience to a householder, who just happened to be the local planning officer. The sound of chainsaws at dawn still brings on feelings of dread in me. But the deeper impact was the realisation that trees could also be objects, separate things, not just by being appropriated as private property or commodities, but in an almost grammatical sense, as the victims of sentences in which we, as humans, were the subjects.

But I'm in no position to feel saintly. I've owned a wood myself, felled trees, sold timber. In the decades that followed my privileged childhood, I guess I went through most of the possible relationships that can exist between trees and humans, coming round, fifty years on, to the point where I started. When I was a teenager I was a tree-hugger, not in some vague, spiritual sense but literally, because I loved their intense physicality in my arms. Later, under the spell of Oliver Rackham's bewitching expeditions into historical ecology, I became a kind of dowser. Wherever I was I'd be on the hunt for ancient woods, browsing old maps for tell-tale boundaries and occult place names, teaching myself the lexicon of plants endemic to these old treelands: the golden coronets of herb paris, the sweetness of sweet woodruff, the magenta flash of red helleborine among the grey trunks of a Cotswold beechwood. These places felt to me like life rafts out of the past. I saw the wood of stunted holly on the shingle of Dungeness, a beachwood first mentioned in an eighth-century charter, and the gargantuan Tortworth chestnut, a single organism whose drooping branches have self-layered until it resembles a small wood.

I guess my entanglement with woods became something of an obsession. But I'm not sure that entirely explains why, in my late thirties, I desperately wanted to have one of my own. Maybe I wanted somewhere to play among the trees again. Maybe I thought I could save one small space from the continued devastation that old woods were suffering and restore some of those ancestral links with human settlement. Whatever the reasons, when one of my books proved lucky, I blew the proceeds on 16 acres of ancient wood near my home in the Chilterns, with the proclaimed intention of turning it into a 'community wood'. What that meant in practice I hadn't really thought through, but I let the community in anyway. E M Forster bought a wood in his middle years, and found that ownership made him feel 'heavy' with an obligation to 'do something with it'.

I experienced those conflicting emotions acutely. I knew intellectually that the wood would thrive even if we did absolutely nothing to it – except it would do it at its own pace, not ours, and I fancied seeing some perceptible evolution in my own lifespan. The conflict at least ensured that nothing as authoritarian as a management plan emerged. I pretty much let anyone who felt attached to the place, from chainsaw-wielders to bat surveyors, get on with whatever they felt appropriate.

The result was as if a small herd of benign herbivores had invaded the wood. Glades emerged in what was at the start a dark and crowded space, overplanted with matchwood poplars. Paths were trodden out along old deer and badger tracks. Kids made trapezes slung hair-raisingly over the old marl-pits, and formed escorts for frogs migrating back to the pond. I added my own ornamentation, responding perhaps to some ancient instinct to fiddle with sticks inherited from our ancestors, and pruned brambles to give the primroses a better show and low branches to form arches over the tracks.

For the twenty years of my ownership (or tenancy, as I preferred to think of it) working and playing in the wood seemed a rewarding and enjoyable experience for everyone, especially the children. What we didn't do was encourage them to artificially plant trees, believing that witnessing the astonishing natural regeneration that began wherever we had let in the light was a more profound lesson. This was just one piece of evidence that the wood seemed to be finding it a positive experience, too, as it began its own agenda of development, partly as a result of our tinkering, partly from its own deep cycles. Holly began springing up in new places, voting itself in as the next shrub-layer. Wood vetch, one of the loveliest and rarest plants in the county, swarmed along the edges of the new tracks. Buzzards returned to nest.

Looking back, I doubt I would have done much different. Accumulating evidence of the autonomy and resilience of tree communities, and the discovery of the 'wood-wide-web'– the underground network of mycorrhizal fungi connecting all the trees – rather vindicates our low level of intervention. We weren't 'managing' the wood (how I hate that term, with its echoes of the biblical 'dominion over nature' that got us into trouble in the first place) but participating in it. I sometimes wonder, in the spirit of reciprocity, how woods might manage us. Would they want us to get out, leave them alone to develop naturally as they did for aeons before we arrived on the scene? Maybe, given what we have done to them. But I hope that they might give us a conditional welcome, as a species evolved in the savanna, indulging our desire to make a congenial niche for ourselves alongside the badgers and bark-beetles.

COMMON GROUND

MANIFESTO *for* TREES

1. Trees need more protection

Trees stand for Nature, and we shall stand or fall with them. Britain is one of the least wooded countries in Europe and we need to keep our trees. Work for the protection of all trees and be vigilant. Make every tree a wanted tree.

2. Stand up for old trees and ancient woods

All old trees and ancient woods are priceless and should be jealously guarded. Old trees are more valuable than young trees, culturally, ecologically and aesthetically. They are a distinguishing characteristic of the British countryside. For some trees life begins at 400.

3. Keep the carbon locked up

Trees breathe in carbon and hold it in their very fibres. We can help keep it there for as long as possible. We should keep trees alive and growing in the first instance, then turn their wood into durable products and finally only burn it as a last resort.

4. Re-use and recycle paper and wood

Each of us consumes more than four trees' worth of paper products every year. Collect, re-use and recycle waste paper at home, in your office and in your neighbourhood.

5. Let trees seed freely

Existing woods could be allowed to expand through natural regeneration by letting trees seed freely and seedlings grow up protected from browsing animals. It just requires some patience.

6. Get behind the hedge

Hedges and hedgerow trees are historically important in our landscape. Some hedges have marked boundaries for a thousand years and are remnants of ancient woods. They give shade, serve as windbreaks, sheltering crops and animals, provide habitats and corridors for wildlife and reduce soil erosion.

7. Think carefully before you plant a tree

We are obsessed with planting trees, yet trees are often planted without thought for what's already there or the views of local people. In towns, a human helping hand can improve tree establishment and survival, especially in streets and where soils are problematic.

8. Grow your own trees

If you do decide to plant, try growing some trees from locally collected seed. By using seed collected locally you can enhance local distinctiveness and preserve local genetic diversity. Growing trees from seed is a great educational project.

9. Grow the right trees in the right place

Different types of tree enjoy particular climatic and soil conditions and have association with different places. The right tree will thrive and endure in the right place. We should grow trees around us that enhance the identity of places and add to local distinctiveness.

10. Grow trees to make places

An individual tree can create a place with beauty, atmosphere and myriad cultural and historical associations. Grow trees which will help to give meaning to a place: for people to congregate, places to muse, avenues to stroll along, landmarks and boundary markers.

11. Welcome wildness

Welcome wildness and discourage overtidiness. Deadwood should be left for wildlife and to add beauty. A fallen tree is not a dead tree: even with only a quarter of its roots left in the ground a 'lateral' tree may survive to produce many new vertical stems.

12. Design new buildings around trees

Thousands of trees are felled to make way for new development each year. Many more are debilitated and die later owing to soil compaction, roots severance and damage to trunk and branch. By retaining existing trees when constructing new buildings, we can add maturity and richness, as well as value, to houses, offices, supermarkets and car parks.

13. Don't axe garden trees

Garden trees are very important, accounting for about a quarter of our non-forest woodland trees. A mature tree brings shade, privacy and birdsong into your garden, as well as enhancing your property. Remember, you are buying a tree with a house in the garden! Tell your neighbours how much you appreciate their trees.

14. Find new uses for old woodland

We need to find new uses for small, deciduous woods, to expand our native hardwood industry and the market for wood products. Working woodlands are more likely to endure. Encourage good traditional practices and search for new ones. Working woodlands are a joy to walk in, too.

15. Save old trees, plant Community Orchards

England has lost more than two-thirds of its orchards since 1950. Yet in traditional tall-tree orchards we and nature together have created a treasury of genetic diversity, beautiful landscapes and a repository of culture. Save old orchards, plant new ones in the city and country. Community Orchards are a wise way of sharing the land and are a fruitful gift to those who follow.

16. Feel the benefit of trees

Simply looking at trees or walking in woods makes us feel better. Trees shield us from pollution, noise and summer heat. They improve the quality of the air we breathe, trapping dust particles and harmful gases.

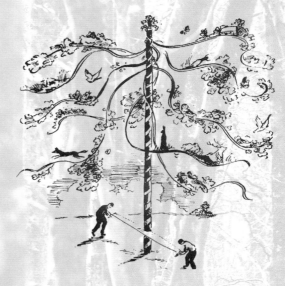

17. Act locally

The destruction of rainforests might seem a distant problem that is beyond our influence and unconnected with what happens in our own localities. It is not. Unless we take more care about where our timber comes from and look after our own trees, how can we honestly urge others to protect theirs? Help the trees in your own place.

18. Celebrate your trees

For Tree Dressing Day (1st weekend in December), share your stories and traditions to invent a festival in which young and old, professional and amateur, all cultures can share. Create a social celebration for the trees in your street or on the green.

19. Make friends with a tree

Trees are not fragile ornaments, but tough, enduring, dependable creatures, if we treat them well. They are our friends and we can learn a tremendous amount from them. Observe a tree from day to day, through the seasons, from decade to decade. Climb a tree, feel its strength, stability, gentle flexing and quietness.

TREES HAVE NO VOICE, WE MUST SPEAK UP FOR THEM

ROOF BOSSES IN THE CLOISTER, NORWICH CATHEDRAL, fourteenth or fifteenth century, from the Kathleen Basford archive

Kathleen Basford (1916–1998) was a British botanist with a special interest in genetics, but was also known for her research into the cultural significance of the Green Man in the British Isles and around the world. In 1978 she published *The Green Man*, a landmark exploration of how the foliate head has been used as an ornament in building since the fourth and fifth centuries, first borrowed from antiquity and modified to express particular ideas and meaning. Basford herself called it the 'spiritual dimension of nature' in architecture.

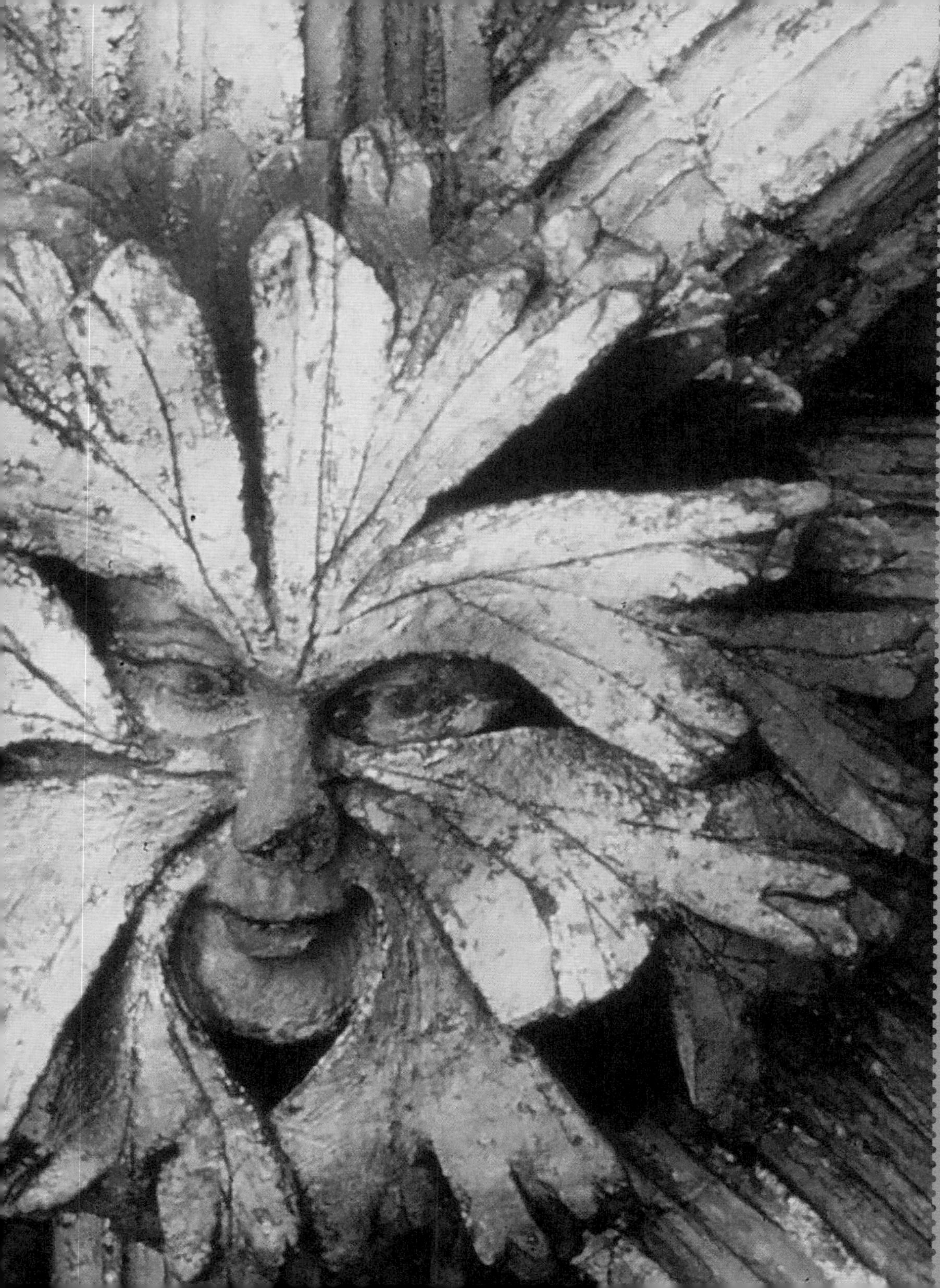

OUT OF THE WILDWOOD

GREEN MAN by Peter Freeman, *Out of the Wood* **exhibition, 1989**

Peter Freeman's neon *Green Man* was included in the exhibition *Out of the Wood*, a collaboration between Common Ground and the Crafts Council, which – through glass, ceramics, sculpture, jewellery, wood-turning, photography, metalwork and neon – explored the vitality of wood as a material and the historic cultural relationship between craft and the natural world. The show opened at London's South Bank in August 1989 and travelled to Barnsley, Middlesborough, Stoke-on-Trent, Leicester, Birmingham, Derby, Kendal, Eastbourne and finally, Aberystwyth, where it closed in 1991.

Wild nature is self-willed: it does what it likes. Yet we seek to control it, until it is tamed, domesticated, still natural but no longer wild. The story of civilisation describes a journey out of the wild, from the forest to the city, which has exploited natural landscapes, subjugated nature and extinguished species along the way. Over the last 11,000 years, the wild has been reduced to a few dominant plants (wheat, maize, spruce) and most of the world's vertebrates are now either human or dependent on humans for their existence (sheep, cows, chickens). Under the reign of *Homo sapiens*, the oceans are awash with plastic, rainforests are being pulped, bushfires are raging, diseases are going global and many wild species, companions on our evolutionary journey, face extinction. We live on a degraded planet, with less natural abundance and biodiversity than there was just 50 years ago.

It's difficult to believe that we were once part of the forest, living among the trees, eating the fruits of the forest, part of its protective matrix. Even before humans arrived on the scene 300,000 years ago, forest had dominated the Earth for 300 million years. Trees, as Richard Mabey reminds us, 'are what dry land aspires to become'. We may have carved out our existence from the forest, but the forest came first. Trees are the natural state. So the real question is, why *not* trees? What have we done to stop trees growing almost everywhere?

Where once there was wildwood, there are now fields of wheat, cows, car parks, housing, industrial zones, power stations, distribution warehouses and data-storage facilities. We keep pushing back the forests, carving out more and more clearings. The remaining trees we tolerate, but only on our terms, only in places we choose, only of approved species and of a size and shape convenient to our needs, only for as long as

WILDWOOD 6-4000 BC

Trees, trees and more trees! Britain is cut off from the continent by rising sea level and our native flora is established. A dynamic patchwork of woodland and grassland in which the grazing of deer and aurochs (wild oxen) play an important part. The first trees to appear after the last Ice Age, 12,000 to 6,000 years ago, were pine and birch, then hazel. Ash appears relatively early but sparsely.

we require. No wonder nature is having a nervous breakdown! And what has it cost us, the oppressors?

Perhaps the truth is that not everyone likes trees. After all, they can be difficult neighbours: getting in the way, growing over our fences and streets, never moving on, growing bigger all the time, dropping leaves where they are not wanted, blocking the view and shading the sun, rooting around in our drains and undermining foundations. Individually, we worry that a branch might fall on the house or on a passer-by. Collectively, forests provide the eerie backdrop to our TV crime dramas and worst nightmares. As a society, we are more likely to mistreat trees than wild birds or mammals – not out of malice but lack of awareness.

Having lost so much tree cover in Britain, it's hard to imagine how a tree-based society could emerge again. But whatever we think of trees, they will always erupt, grow through the cracks, push up along the edgelands, by streams, in field boundaries, quietly pursuing life. And people will always join them, resisting the suppression of nature and finding imaginative ways to nurture an unofficial countryside inside the towns and cities, by planting orchards on derelict land, starting community firewood groups and suburban forest schools, or planting avenues of trees and hedges around school sports fields.

We once thought that subjugating all that wilderness would protect our own little patch, but it turns out we are all woven of the same cloth. We *are* the fabric of nature. We are *part* of the web of life, so we need wildness in order to support our own lives. There have been massive gains for human societies from the exploitation of nature, but now we are seeing the (not so hidden) costs: the global climate is disrupted and ecosystems are in a state of collapse. We face challenges of food supply, fresh water, pollution, pandemic, wildfire and population growth. Responses to this rapid breakdown need to be comprehensive and swift. The science tells us we *must* change; technology tells us we *can* change; it is now up to us to declare that we *will* change.

So what would it take to live closer to trees, woods and nature again? Is it possible to restore forest cover and thriving wildlife? Can an urban-dwelling, twenty-first century population develop an authentic wood culture?

Today, trees and woods mean many different things to different

people. They can be a stand of timber, a precious wildlife habitat, an ecosystem 'service provider', a place of learning, a source of inspiration filled with nature spirits and stories. The protection of our remaining trees and any ambitious plan to restore the treed landscape must begin by understanding the meaning of trees – because it is through the trees and woods that we'll find the metaphorical and practical tools that we need to live and work in closer balance with nature. When we look around us, as we do in this book, it's heartening to discover so many inspiring ideas and hopeful signs. Our journey back towards the trees begins with these compelling stories about the restoration of our place in nature.

Rising up: author and campaigner Dara McAnulty (front centre) with fellow students at Youth Strike for Climate gathering in Belfast, Northern Ireland, in September 2019 – one of many events expressing the great groundswell of emotion and urgency for change around the world. Photograph by Róisín McAnulty.

Our modus vivendi with trees

Equal rights for woods! *Vote tree. #Treestoo.*

Too often we think of what benefits trees and woods offer us. Instead, it's high time we asked what *we* can offer the trees. Luckily, there's a growing appetite for expressing this shift in thinking, particularly in a younger generation of naturalists and activists, interconnected by social media, who recognise the urgency in speaking out for nature.

SWEET TRACK 3806 BCE
A two-kilometre trackway across the wetlands of the Somerset Levels is built out of long oak planks with pieces of hazel, alder, ash, holly, willow and coppiced lime. Coppicing – the cutting and re-cutting of small underwood shoots from the base of a tree – is a lynchpin of traditional woodland management to this day. Neolithic woodsmanship was very sophisticated, crafting different sizes of different woods without the use of metal tools.

All over the UK people are forging new relationships with trees and woods. There is much to learn from these exceptional individuals and communities: their example shows us the way, and we can all play our part in shaping a culture that puts nature at the centre of life and the decisions we make about the future.

We have destroyed so much of our natural home for too long, but Common Ground believes that a new 'wood culture' is possible. By exploring the inspiring ways in which people are living with trees, we can demonstrate how human social and economic renewal can exist *within* nature. It is up to us to find new ways to value and celebrate the trees in our lives. As this book will show, we must not wait for successive governments, political leaders or policies to do it for us. We have to show them the way.

Trees are the natural state

Some 12,000 years ago, as the ice sheets were retreating during the last Ice Age, trees gradually recolonised the newly revealed land. This included the British Isles, which were still connected to Continental Europe by a land bridge known as Doggerland.

Soon came the pioneer species: willow and birch, their light seeds able to germinate on bare land and endure climatic hardships of cold, wet and wind. Then came Scots pine and hazel, followed by oak, alder, lime, elm and ash. Last to arrive were beech and hornbeam. As global temperatures continued to rise (and ice continued to melt), the lowlands of Doggerland disappeared under the encroaching waves of the North Sea. Around 8,000 years ago (6,000 BCE) Britain became an island.

There is still debate amongst ecologists about how much forest covered these islands. For many years the idea of 'wildwood' was one of an endless closed-canopy forest covering most of the land. But this view has been challenged by Hans Vera, the Dutch ecologist, who proposes a more open mosaic of trees and glades, regulated by megafauna – cattle (aurochs), elk, boar and wild horses – which grazed a landscape resembling savanna.

This forest cover – continuous or mosaic – lasted until about 3,800 BCE: the dawn of the Neolithic age, when agriculture arrived from the Fertile Crescent in the Middle East. Instead of

natural selection governing the distribution of species, as it had done for billions of years, humans started 'artificially' selecting plants and animals to suit their needs, and set about expressing a preference for the kind of landscape that suited them. This also meant choosing where trees were allowed to grow.

The balance was tipped, and as a more settled agricultural population expanded, the influence of the landscape retreated even further. Although we can imagine a time when the landscape was the most significant determining factor of human activity, shaping what could be built, grown, made and

Wistman's Wood on Dartmoor is an ecological jewel, full of gnarled and stunted oak, dripping with mosses and lichens, protected by huge mossy boulders. This upland oakwood has survived here for centuries, possibly a remnant of the original wildwood.

traded, this relationship has now completely reversed. It is the will of human economy that drives our society, which in turn determines what we do with different landscapes.

So what trees have we lost and what remains? Historic choices of land use have continued to push back the forest: by the beginning of the twentieth century, only 4.7 per cent of the British Isles was covered in trees. By comparison, the average cover on the Continent is currently around 38 per cent, with France and Germany enjoying 30 per cent. This has fluctuated, though, and it is not just the UK that has had low forest cover: all the flat fertile lowlands of north-western Europe have been cultivated for agriculture, whereas the less fertile and more difficult land to farm, such as the mountainous parts of southern and central Europe, have retained trees. Even the Scandinavian countries, much revered for their forests and wood culture, enjoy varied forest cover: Norway (40 per cent), Sweden (68 per cent), Finland (73 per cent) and Denmark (14 per cent).

Remnants of wildwood

The pioneering botanical writer Oliver Rackham identified a number of 'wildwood provinces' thought to have been growing in the British Isles around 4500 BCE: south-east England dominated by lime; south-west England, Wales, northern England and southern Scotland favouring oak and hazel; pine found in the Scottish Highlands and birch in the far north. Of these native forests only about 1 per cent now remains.

This is a massive vanishing, yet the remnants are a wonderfully biodiverse natural heritage. They are completely unique and irreplaceable. They have experienced generations of use and abuse, and are still under threat. These Ancient Semi-Natural Woodlands (or ASNWs) are dotted across the UK and reflect the local geology, soils, topography and climate in their species composition, and often bear witness to a long history of human intervention.

In the Scottish Highlands the Caledonian Pinewoods form a distinctive community, often with birch and other broadleaved trees. The native pines develop great billowing canopies when allowed to mature, quite unlike plantation pines. There has been

Photograph by Paul Moody

HISTORIC WOODS

Fingle Woods is an 655-acre ancient woodland site in the Teign Valley on the northern fringes of Dartmoor National Park in Devon. Over millennia, tides of history have swept across the landscape, leaving glimpses into the lives of local people utilising the wood for timber, coppice, tanbark, shelter and feeding livestock.

During the Bronze and Iron Ages people settled on the high promontories of Fingle Woods, where they hunted and foraged. This occupation was followed by the development of complex land ownership and rights exercised for livestock, fuel and building materials, some of which is recorded in the Domesday Book. In the eighteenth and nineteenth centuries, the rural economy changed significantly and the role of woods shifted, embodied by the term used to map areas of moribund coppice: 'waste'.

This decline was followed by renewal following the First World War, led by the philanthropist and visionary Leonard Elmhirst who owned the Dartington Estate. He acquired the woodlands in the early part of the twentieth century and set about the conversion of the 'waste' to a conifer silviculture under the guidance of renowned forestry academic Wilfred Hiley. The plan was to revive the rural economy from the post-war Depression of the 1930s and to create employment.

Despite their drive and passion, the 'Forestry Venture' fell into decline in the 1960s, just as the conifer trees were beginning to mature. Fingle was sold into a pension fund, under which began a programme of clearfelling, while much of the remaining mature conifer succumbed to the storms of the 1990s. The woods were replanted, but they faced the combined challenges of 'making it pay' with young crops, faltering markets and the cyclical nature of clearfell silviculture.

Through some good fortune, the Woodland Trust and National Trust were able to acquire the site in 2013 with the support of local people. It may take at least 100 years, but the restoration of this Plantation on an Ancient Woodland Site (PAWS) is a continuation of the philanthropy of the Elmhirsts, creating local employment and reconnecting the woods to the lives of the local community (*see* pages 144–145).

However, tree disease, the observed loss of species on Dartmoor and the emerging impacts of the changing climate are now ever-present. These deep valley woodlands provide stable refugia where some of our most iconic but most threatened woodland species might continue to thrive.

Beechwood in the New Forest, Hampshire. Here beechwood has formed on sands and gravels, as at Burnham Beeches, though beechwoods also thrive on chalk soils in the Chilterns. Photograph by Adrian Newton.

little regeneration of these woods until recently (*see* Mar Lodge on pages 201–202), so they tend to be missing the intermediate generations between the elders and the new growth.

Elsewhere in the northern and western uplands of Britain, there are distinctive stands of birchwoods, oakwoods and ashwoods. Birch is a hardy tree of poor soils and is often joined by oak and hazel, with rowan on more acidic soils (Scotland's Highland birchwoods are particularly splendid). 'Upland ashwoods' prefer richer, less acidic soils, again with oak and often elm and lime, also with sycamore colonising. They support a rich ecosystem of flowers, invertebrates and lichen. They can be found throughout upland Britain and in Northern Ireland, with notable stands in the Derbyshire Dales and the Mendips.

Sessile oak dominates the upland oakwoods, and downy birch is also frequent in the canopy. On richer flushes, ash and elm might be present too, whilst boggy areas tend towards alder. Common in Argyll, Cumbria, Gwynedd and also the higher ground of Devon and Cornwall, these woods support particularly rich communities of ferns, mosses and liverworts, woodland birds and insects. The south of England, from East Anglia across to Bristol and down to the Channel, is known to ecologists as the Beech Zone, thought to be the natural range of beech when it migrated north after the last Ice Age. Here beech grows on acid, neutral and alkaline soils. Beechwoods are very familiar on the ridges of the chalk Downs and on the limestones of the Chilterns and Cotswolds. Other trees common in these woods are ash, sycamore, yew and whitebeam. Neutral and heavier soils are more often found with oak and holly. The most acidic beechwoods are found on sands and gravels, again with holly and oak, most famously in the New Forest and Burnham Beeches.

Lowland woods not dominated by beech are known as lowland mixed broadleaved woods, and they grow on a wide range of soils and locations, often as well-defined islands in a matrix of surrounding farmland. These include the classic ancient coppice woodlands of oak, ash, field maple and hazel on the richer soils, and wood pastures of oak and birch on more acid sands. Traditional coppice management practices have usually been abandoned in these places, resulting in woods growing into high forest during the twentieth century, with sycamore and sweet chestnut as common colonisers.

Throughout all of Britain there are also Wet Woodlands dominated by alder and willow, found on a wide range of soils. They often form small stands within these other woodlands, grading into birch, ash and oak where they meet drier land. The moist conditions favour mosses and liverworts in particular.

Wood Pasture is a very valuable and rare woodland type, and more an example of traditional management than a reflection of its specific location. Its value lies in the rich mosaic of habitats, including high forest, ancient trees, scrubland and meadows, all kept in dynamic equilibrium by grazing animals. The New Forest, Windsor Great Park, Epping Forest and Glen Finglas in Scotland are notable examples of ancient wood pastures.

SWEET CHESTNUT 55 CE
Originally from southern Europe, western Asia and north Africa, this broadleaf tree arrived on these shores with the Roman Empire, perhaps brought with the legions who breakfasted on porridge made from sweet chestnut. Roman Britain saw little change in woodland area (20 per cent)

THE ANKERWYCKE YEW
Anglo-Saxons colonise Britain: possibly a modest increase in woodland to about 25 per cent. Trees were sacred to the Anglo-Saxons and Vikings. Witans, or King's Councils, were often held under important trees. Alfred the Great (Wessex King 871 - 899 AD) held Witans at Runnymede, possibly under the branches of the Ankerwycke Yew, which took root at Runnymede around 2,000 years ago. This tree still stands here today.

Ancient woods

The wildwood mosaic of forests, glades, marshes, bogs and thickets which once covered our land has been picked away over the millennia, dug up, paved over, leaving only a few scattered pieces as clues to the former pattern. They are now isolated, ancient fragments that have miraculously survived the centuries in the hard and straight edges of the humanscape.

Ancient woods are officially defined as any wood that has been in existence since 1600 in England, Wales and Northern Ireland or 1750 in Scotland. Before this time, tree planting was not common, so it is reckoned that any woodland on the map at that date would have been there for some considerable time and evolved naturally. In these islands almost all woods have been modified in some way by humans, so these ancient woods are only partly 'natural', hence the term Ancient Semi-Natural Woodland.

As these places have been wooded for so long, the soils have usually never been ploughed, or not in recent historical time, so they are alive with a teeming soil ecosystem of their own which we are only now beginning to discover; this in turn plays a hugely significant role in tree health and supports a range of flora not found on disturbed soils or on more recently planted sites.

Ancient woods were often enclosed from the 'wastes' in mediaeval times and protected from grazing animals because of their valuable wood products. They were then worked intensively over the centuries – both the coppice understorey and the timber overstorey – with more valuable species favoured to produce a highly modified 'semi-natural' structure and habitat. The periodic influx of light and disturbance has generated a characteristic flora and fauna, which is lost when the coppicing stops. The actual age of the trees in an ancient wood is not the crucial factor – it is the time the whole woodland site has been wooded and the soils undisturbed. Of course, there are often trees of great antiquity in ancient woods, which adds to their natural value.

The British ecologist John Lawton, when he published the independent review, *Making Space for Nature*, compared ancient woods to ancient cathedrals or churches: originating in mediaeval times, a focus for community life through the

NEW FOREST 1079
Following the Norman Conquest, the New Forest was proclaimed a royal forest by William the Conqueror. It was created from over 20 hamlets and isolated farmsteads, becoming a single, 'new' area. Domesday Book recorded 15 per cent woodland cover in England, with the biggest concentrations in the Sussex Weald and the Chiltern plateau.

Rainforest can be found here in the UK on the west coast, where there is high rainfall and humidity. Also known as Atlantic Woodland or Coastal Temperate Rainforest, these are often oakwoods with birch, ash and hazel, supporting a very rich flora of mosses, lichens and liverworts. They are sometimes threatened by invasive rhododendron. Photograph of Merthen Middle Pill, Cornwall, by Oliver Rackham, courtesy of Jenny Moody.

Upland birchwoods in Scotland are widespread on acid and infertile soils, dominated by downy birch with some rowan, sessile oak and pine. Juniper sometimes occurs as an understorey.

centuries, altered, enlarged, diminished, but always rooted in the same spot, shaped by time and place. There is a finite number of these cultural artefacts: faith and use have waned over the last century, so many lie in disrepair. We can begin to make new ones, more suited to our current tastes and adapted to the challenges we face, but it would surely be sacrilege to allow these unique places to be destroyed.

Ancient woods are too important – ecologically and culturally – for their fate to be left to market forces or cost-benefit analysis. So how should we look after our ancient woods? The first thing, of course, is doing everything in our power to stop them being destroyed by immediate threats. It sounds simple but woods are often viewed as soft options when space is needed for 'development' of houses, roads, railways or quarries. It is also important to intervene to free ancient woods from the choking grip of rhododendron and the hungry mouths of deer.

In February 2017, the Woodland Trust reported over 700 ancient woods under threat from development, with the High Speed 2 (HS2) rail project identified as the single biggest threat: 108 ancient woods facing loss or damage along the proposed routes, with 32 ancient woods directly affected and a further 29 to suffer secondary effects during Phase 1 of the scheme linking London to Birmingham. There may be compensatory planting efforts for new woods, but this entirely misunderstands the unique value of ancient woods which simply cannot be replaced.

To address the threat from HS2 and other forms of inappropriate development, the Woodland Trust is campaigning for protection of ancient woods in national planning policy, similar to that protecting listed buildings. There has even been some success: the 2018 National Planning Policy Framework (NPPF) now only allows damage or destruction of ancient wood in 'wholly exceptional circumstances'. But this policy framework does not apply to any projects that are considered 'national infrastructure', such as HS2.

The law is being increasingly used to protect our natural world, such as the landmark ruling that the third runway at Heathrow airport was inconsistent with plans for net zero carbon by 2050; HS2 has been (unsuccessfully) challenged in the courts by Chris Packham for its destructive impact on wildlife, woods and the

Above: Kingsettle Wood (Woodland Trust) near Shaftesbury in Dorset; a Plantation on Ancient Woodland Site (or PAWS) still with displays of wild garlic and bluebells.

Left: Also known as Fox Covert, Glyn Davies Wood, Northamptonshire, is one of the many irreplaceable ancient woods under threat from the HS2 rail link. Photograph by Philip Formby, courtesy of the Woodland Trust.

FOREST OF DEAN
From the 1600s an increased demand for oak timber for shipbuilding and tan-bark prompted John Evelyn to write 'Sylva, or Discourse of Forest-Trees and the Propagation of Timber'. Publication of the book marked the beginning of modern forestry, with woods planted or managed for specific markets. But the supply of timber was no better 150 years later when Horatio Nelson wrote 'The State of the Forest at this moment is deplorable'. In the Forest of Dean, he believed that the cultivation of oak 'would produce about 9,200 loads of timber fit for building Ships'. As a result of Nelson's intervention, 30 million acorns were planted in the Forest!

climate. Could this be the moment we realise the existential importance of the climate and ecological emergency?

As a society, we obviously accord a far greater value to our own artefacts and ancient buildings than to these cathedrals of the natural world. In our modern age of concrete, steel and plastic, trees and woods remain under threat because we simply don't value them highly enough.

Ancient trees

We have lost much of our ancient woodland, yet because of our cultural history we are unusually well endowed with ancient trees compared to the rest of Europe: there are an estimated 3,400 oaks over 400 years old in Britain, compared to 1,260 in Sweden and 800 in the rest of Continental Europe. When the Normans invaded in 1066, all the land belonged to the new King William, who kept some and divided the rest amongst his nobles. The king and the nobles imported fallow deer and set up hunting parks, called 'Forests' and 'Chases'. These were not heavily wooded areas, but rather open parkland where you could first see the deer and then chase them on horseback. Along with protecting the deer, these playgrounds of the nobility also conserved their habitat, which meant that individual oak trees were protected from the commoners' axe. About half of the ancient oaks in England can be traced to these Norman hunting parks.

Protection is essential for trees to become ancient – because it takes time. There are few things slower than ancient trees, and they do make a huge and unique contribution to the biodiversity and character of places. Ancient trees have accrued features, experience and niches through the ages that provide the architecture for a vast community of other plants and animals. They are living ecosystems in their own right – there are species of beetle and fungi which will live nowhere else but the decaying heart of old trees. They truly are pillars of the community. Those that remain have been rooted to the same spot as human epochs pass, surviving the plough, the mechanisation of farming and then the industrialisation of agriculture and the associated chemical and hedge clearances.

WOOD-WIDE-WEB

We have known how mycorrhizal fungi form associations with tree roots for a long time, but we are only just beginning to discover the connection and communication between trees.

Fungal threads (or hyphae) are collectively called mycelium, and vast networks of these are absorbing nutrients from the soil and sharing with trees. It's a symbiotic relationship: trees receive nutrients such as nitrogen and phosphorus, while fungi receive sugars from the trees (up to 20 per cent of photosynthates from trees flow into the fungi). This network of fungal threads spreads out across the whole forest floor, acting as a 'safety net' to prevent nutrients from leaching away.

By tracking radioactive isotopes under controlled conditions, the forest ecologist Suzanne Simard discovered transfer of carbon between trees, even of different species. This revolutionises our view of the forest. No longer is it just a place of competition for light and space and nutrients, but also an example of co-operation in nature, with the individual members of the forest community working as a superorganism.

These communities of trees have busy hubs — or 'mother trees' — which actively nurture the young trees with carbon and defence signals. Although the forest has a great capacity to self-heal, removing hub trees can have a catastrophic effect on the health of the forest as a whole — especially ancient woods.

We have been told we struggle to survive in a world of 'dog-eat-dog', but it might be more accurate to say we co-exist in a network of 'tree-feed-tree'. This has huge implications for the way we manage forests, treat trees and understand ourselves within nature.

Our interventions in the forest can be highly destructive, both above and below ground. Mycorrhizae can be damaged by soil disturbance, compaction and chemicals (including excessive nitrogen), and a tree's connections are severed by ploughs or excavators.

As we learn more about forest ecology, we need to reconsider our impact on the forest and find ways of preserving its overall integrity. We can plant trees, but we cannot plant a forest. A forest will only evolve over time as the individual components are woven together into a superorganism.

How little we know! Before we plan any more grand schemes that intervene in nature, perhaps we need to be humble about the complexity of forests and trees. Only then will we start to tread more carefully when it comes to making plans for nature.

Training volunteers to record trees, such as this yew tree at Breamore, Hampshire, for the Ancient Tree Inventory. The Ancient Tree Hunt is a programme run by the Ancient Tree Forum. Any member of the public can record trees they consider ancient, veteran or notable and submit their findings. The result is a map of Britain populated by over 120,000 trees, each recorded and measured.

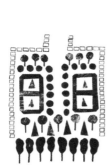

ORNAMENTAL
PLANTING 1700s
Landowners start to make new ornamental parks and plantations, to enclose and reorganise the countryside, but many ancient woods managed through woodsmanship also survive.

They have 'witnessed' wars, survived droughts, boring beetles and fungal attacks, and not least dodged the axe and chainsaw. Whilst there are many tales of wildlife woe, ancient and veteran trees have prospered. They give us hope.

Our recent recognition of ancient, veteran and notable trees is a heartening example of how we can value, understand and care for trees. However, many still go unnoticed and suffer damage and destruction. We also need to find and protect a new generation of potential ancient and veteran trees. As with ancient woods, there is a legal mechanism that enables us to help protect trees, called Tree Preservation Orders (*see* page 63). Unfortunately, our ability to protect individual ancient trees has been hugely undermined recently: according to the Woodland Trust, the 2018 National Planning Policy Framework 'separates ancient woodland from aged and veteran trees, essentially lowering the status of these incredible natural monuments by setting out in the text that aged and veteran trees are not irreplaceable habitats.'

Despite the political pledges and widespread enthusiasm for planting millions of trees to 'fight' climate change, this sad truth reveals the shocking neglect of our arboreal elders. Surely it is time to express our commitment to nature by enshrining in law the protection of any irreplaceable organism or habitat, above and beyond human needs.

Veteran ash hedge in Dorset (*top*), no longer maintained as a field boundary. The horizontal stems were once plashed or laid, which has given the tree 'veteran' features: a lost limb, dead branches, a hollow trunk. Old ash pollards, such as these (*bottom right*) languishing in the depths of a forestry plantation in Dyffryn Crawnon, often originated on boundary walls in farmland and are typical of those in highland regions of England and Wales. Both are examples of veteran trees because they have developed features that are not the result of age but experience and the local growing environment. Similarly, this lime tree growing in a Shaftesbury churchyard (*bottom left*), although a relatively young 120 years for its species, has developed features that will grow in ecological interest as the tree ages and accumulate layers of cultural association.

A century of planting

Planting is all the rage these days but it isn't new. Over the last century, ambitious afforestation (planting on new land) expanded UK forest cover from the dismal 4.7 per cent of 1900 to about 13 per cent today. The extent of afforestation has varied across the land: England has moved from about 5 per cent to 10 per cent, Wales from 5 per cent to 15 per cent, Scotland from 5 per cent to 18 per cent and Northern Ireland from 1 per cent to 8 per cent.

All this sounds like good news but there's much to learn from the mistakes of the last century of planting. We must also remember that these newly planted trees and forests in no way compensate for the ancient woods that have been lost.

After the First World War, it wasn't sparse tree cover or climate disruption that prompted tree planting. It was the lack of timber to support the war effort that led to the government building a 'strategic reserve' of timber for the nation. This was state intervention on a huge scale, and led to the Forestry Act of 1919 and the formation of the Forestry Commission (a governmental department that started to buy land for planting in the 1920s and 1930s). The result was large-scale planting of uplands with exotic conifer species, such as Sitka spruce, larch and lodgepole pine.

The uplands were chosen because the land was cheaper to buy and more readily available; conifers were chosen because they grow fast and uniformly straight, ideal for industrial production; exotic because Sitka spruce from North America grows much faster and in much less fertile areas than our native Scots pine. But even before the new upland forests were ready, the Second World War put more pressure on forests, so the Forestry Commission continued afforestation in the post-war years with renewed vigour.

In the 1960s, a new breed of private forestry company emerged and devised investment schemes for afforestation: planting trees became a way to legally avoid tax whilst investing in an asset. At the time, tax rates were as high as 90 per cent, so there were massive savings to be made and significant amounts of money flowed out of the City of London to buy land and support industrial-scale afforestation. This was an epic scale of

An ancient lime tree growing in Castle Hill Deer Park, Ryedale, North Yorkshire. Ancient trees include trees of great age and size, often hundreds or even thousands of years old, but also trees that are relatively old or large for their species and in the third and final stage of life. An ancient oak tree might have a girth of three 'hugs', while an apple tree or a short-lived birch would be considered ancient with a girth of just one hug.

Trees don't need to be veteran or ancient to be special. A 'notable' tree can be a young or old tree that has become important locally. A black poplar tree bedecked in flags (*right*) was at the centre of the Shropshire village of Aston-on-Clun. Known as the Arbor Tree, the first records of it being decorated date back to May 1786. The Ding Dong tree (*above*) at Prestonpans Primary School, East Lothian, is a copper beech that gets its name from a game invented by pupils who compete to touch its trunk shouting 'ding dong!'. Beloved by generations of pupils, the Ding Dong tree has become central to the life and identity of the school. Photograph courtesy of the Woodland Trust.

intervention again, but this time led by the private sector rather than the state: 1 million hectares (ha) of land were planted between 1960 and 1988 (bear in mind that a grand total of 1.6 million ha were planted between 1900 to 2010, with planting at a rate of up to 30,000 ha per year).

All this planting certainly got a lot of trees growing and created a vast resource, just now coming to maturity. But the planting of conifer forests also led to the loss of some valuable habitats and created many geometric blots on the landscape. Numerous ancient woods were ploughed up, felled or poisoned and replanted with fast-growing exotic conifers, such as Norway spruce, Japanese larch, Douglas fir and Western hemlock. Others were planted with uniform crops of beech or mixtures of spruce and oak. Oliver Rackham described this period of planting from

SAVE VERNON: A NEW GENERATION OF TREES TO PROTECT

Thousands of trees were condemned by Sheffield City Council to 'improve' the conditions of the city's roads and pavements, including Vernon (*above*), a 150-year-old oak tree on Vernon Road, which was reported to be 'a very fine specimen' by the Sheffield Independent Tree Panel, 'with a further 150 years' life.' Despite this, there being no 'strong arboricultural case for retaining this tree,' the City Council insisted it had to go because it was 'causing problems' to private property and there was a risk of legal action. People were outraged and protested passionately. On Valentine's Day, they dressed Vernon with banners and red love hearts adorned with poems and messages. Somebody even wrote a love song for Vernon!

PLANTATION
FORESTRY 1800s
Plantation forestry
starts in earnest, based
on the German model
with a commitment to
conifers and inspired
by 'Empire Forestry'
in British India.
Afforestation of open
land such as moors and
heaths starts.

COMMONS
PRESERVATION 1850
Lord of Loughton encloses
1,000 acres of Epping
Forest, leaving just nine
acres for the villagers.
Thomas Willingale, a
labourer, leads a revolt
and lops hornbeam
pollards for firewood.
The Willingale family
are sentenced to hard
labour but the Commons
Preservation Society takes
up their cause and the
Lord of Loughton is
ordered to remove the
fences. When they refuse
to obey the court ruling,
5,000 people turn
up to protest.

the 1950s as the 'locust years' because ancient woods were 'destroyed at a rate probably never seen before'.

Not all planting is good planting. The uniform plantation perpetuates a cultural attitude to nature: of control and domination. There is something abstract about many of these plantations – they seem strangely detached from their surroundings, not arising from the particular circumstances of the place or the people. Rather, their simple shapes betray their origins on a drawing board, serving distant cash funds and distant policies.

This opportunistic afforestation could not last. By the 1980s, the easily available land had all been planted up, and in Wales and Scotland fierce competition for the remaining land drove prices up. The last frontier for planting was the cheaper lowland peat of the Flow Country in northern Scotland, which also ground to a halt in a clash with bird conservation groups. Then, in 1988, the tax loophole was closed by the Conservative government of the time. The boom era of investment afforestation was over. Planting rates plummeted, and have dropped even further to 5,000–10,000 hectares in recent years.

In response to this post-war planting, cultural attitudes to trees and woods started to shift in the 1970s and 1980s, with the founding of the Woodland Trust (1972) and the Forestry Commission's 'Broadleaves Policy' (1985), which allocated state subsidies to 'maintain and increase the broadleaved woodland ... for a wide range of objectives and giving special attention to Ancient Semi-Natural Woodlands to maintain their special features.' It also became illegal to grub out hedges and broadleaved woods for agriculture, or to replace them with conifers. As a result, conifer planting declined and broadleaf planting rose from 1,000 hectares per year in 1985 to 10,500 hectares in 2000, boosted further still by more widespread public awareness of environmental issues.

During this time, the original remit of the Forestry Commission to plant a national timber reserve evolved into a variety of tasks: job creation in the forestry sector, reducing the UK's enormous timber imports, making money, providing information on pests and diseases, providing public amenity and enhancing wildlife habitat. And alongside changes in the

Forestry Commission, new sources of funding for trees and woods have emerged through private ownership and public subscriptions to charities such as the Woodland Trust. More recently, planting programmes have developed around 'carbon funding', an idea now backed by the Forestry Commission's Woodland Carbon Code assurance scheme and Woodland Carbon Fund. Since the 1990s, the Community Forests movement has also led to planting around London, Bristol, Swindon, the West and East Midlands, and across a belt from Liverpool and Manchester to East Yorkshire. Meanwhile, the National Forest (spread over 200 square miles across Derbyshire, Leicestershire and Staffordshire) has increased tree cover in that area from 6 to 19 per cent.

The forests of the twenty-first century are clearly quite different from the wildwood and the remnants of ancient woods. These new forests are still too young for us to be able to judge their qualities fully. What will Sitka spruce plantations look like in 500 years' time? Perhaps they will be barren hillsides depleted of nutrients and soil, or maybe they will be fully integrated into the landscape and teeming with their own distinctive wildlife.

Harvesting in an industrial Sitka spruce plantation in the Scottish Borders.

FIRST WORLD WAR
1914–1918
The First World War creates a sudden demand for home-grown timber to support the war effort: for building trenches, making weapons.

AFTER 6,000 YEARS OF DEFORESTATION AND A CENTURY OF PLANTING, WHAT IS LEFT?

3,187,000 hectares (ha) of woodland in the UK, covering 13 per cent of the land.

Of this, 1.6 million ha (51 per cent) is conifer (both native pine and exotic plantations) and 1.5 million ha (49 per cent) is broadleaf.

Of the 1.5 million ha of broadleaf woodland, about 645,000 ha (43 per cent) is semi-natural.

Of this, 329,000 ha are Ancient Semi-Natural Woodlands. These 'ASNWs' are the jewels of woodland wildlife and history, yet are only about 10 per cent of total woodland in the UK, or just 1 per cent of land.

Nature is complex and full of surprises! And what will become of all the latest promises to plant?

Today, the urge to plant trees is resurgent. Trees have even become militarised in the language used by campaigners and charities that seek to 'fight' or 'combat' climate change. Trees are popular with politicians, too, with political parties of every hue showing us their green credentials by pledging new forests and millions more trees. But the twentieth century has taught us that planting can go wrong. Why we plant and where, what species and how we care for them must be carefully considered before we start digging holes in the ground. And remember, we can plant trees but we cannot plant a forest. A forest evolves over time as the individual components are woven together into a superorganism, below and above the ground.

Restoring the Balance

The living world is a web of interactions. All creatures and plants are engaged in complex patterns of exchange and support. The health and stability of the whole depends on the health of functioning parts. Diversity is resilience. So although the

SECOND WORLD WAR
1939–1945
The outbreak of war created further sudden demand for home-grown timber and the new Forestry Commission plantations are not ready

Is all tree-planting good planting? This late-twentieth-century 'broadleaf' plantation, with discarded plastic tree guards and many damaged trees, demonstrates that good intentions can often end in neglect.

POST-WAR
'DEVELOPMENT'
Driven by conversion to forestry, expansion of farmland, new roads and urban development, the Forestry Commission actively encourages grubbing up of ancient woodlands and replanting with fast-growing non-native conifers. Stumps of coppice are sprayed with herbicides. This destruction peaks in the 1950s and 1960s. These are the 'locust years'. Also new conifer plantations are put in place in the uplands, funded by favourable tax regimes.

woodpeckers and orchids may seem far removed and irrelevant to our busy lives, we are enmeshed with them in a living network, and their presence or absence is telling us something important about the state of the real world around us.

Humans have been reducing tree cover for thousands of years, and we are now beginning to pay the price. Our ancestors may have inhabited a world of seasonal cycles, a steady state of birth, growth, decay and rebirth. But even our hunter-gatherer ancestors, with their healthier diets and deeper relationship with the natural world, over-exploited the low-hanging fruits of the forest to feed themselves, driving Europe's megafauna – aurochs, mammoths, cave bears – to extinction.

Tree damage is just one aspect of our domination of nature, but it is a key one: it is clear that continued deforestation is related to the multiple crises of climate change, pollution and mass extinction that we now face. Our civilisation cannot continue down this path. Creative change is needed. We can acknowledge

Crickhowell in Powys, Wales, was cut off by the River Usk in February 2020. The increasing frequency and damage caused by flood events should teach us to rethink flood management. Historically, we have straightened rivers and drained the upper catchments, constructed engineered flood defences and funded dredging in the lower catchments. The focus needs to shift towards 'natural flood management' across catchments that seek to restore the whole landscape – including trees – and slow the flow.

the gains of modern life but must also recognise and repair the damage we've done on our long journey from the wildwood.

Until now, the Earth has been bountiful enough to provide a seemingly endless supply of food, water and materials for us. The early extinctions of megafauna would not have bothered the hunter-gatherers because there were always other animals to hunt; the loss of topsoil just meant early farmers moved on to another patch; the infinite air and the vast oceans could surely swallow all our waste?

Not any more. The acceleration of the global economy in the last 70 years has brought us right up against the limits of what is sustainable on Earth. The WWF's Living Planet Index, which tracks population abundance of thousands of vertebrate species, shows an overall decline of 68 per cent in population sizes between 1970 and 2020. Just take a moment to let that sink in. In a single human lifetime, two-thirds of the world's wildlife has gone.

How can we comprehend this loss?

The web of life is dwindling, some threads are strained to breaking point, others have already broken. The more threadbare the safety net, the more vulnerable we all are. Every extinction is another thread broken forever. We have cherry-picked from nature (grain, meat, fibres, fuel), but we cannot continue to treat the natural world like a shopping aisle of produce for our use. Our degraded landscapes already bear witness to centuries of these choices. A wider ecological and social restoration is possible – as Kate Raworth describes in *Doughnut Economics* – if people take what they need ('the social foundation') within the limits of nature ('the ecological ceiling').

Perhaps we are also searching for a way to restore the balance between the wild and the civilised in ourselves, in our families, in our communities. If we let trees and woods emerge where once we have suppressed them, we'll also be expressing the wilder parts of ourselves: where we came from, how we want to live in future.

Abernethy National Nature Reserve (RSPB) in the Cairngorms National Park, consisting of 'Granny Pines' some 200 years old, with natural regeneration of Scots pine popping up through the heather.

HASTINGS TREE MAP by Eleanor Taylor,
commissioned & published for *LEAF!* **newspaper, 2017**

How do you feel about the city's trees? Which are your
favourites? Trees are our neighbours and wherever they
face threat from pollution, disease or unnecessary felling,
a tree map can be used as a tool to express the importance
of trees in the community.

palm tree
outside my
studio

bay tree
from our
garden

leaf from
the Jack

burn it
on the
eve of
next
May day

jack in
the green - a
hastings
tradition. the
jack is
paraded
through the
streets before
being stripped
of its leaves

the trees up
here are
shaped by
the wind

OLD
TOWN

EAST
HILL

key puzzle
my street
one of the
door to my
d home.

WEST HILL

cherry
blossom
from outside
cafe

STINGS TREE MAP

CITY TREE by Romy Blümel, commissioned and published for *LEAF!* newspaper, 2016

We need to hold our precious trees in a loving embrace, especially when they find themselves alone in the city, isolated from the support network of other trees and wildlife.

We come across trees in our lives every day and mostly take them for granted. Trees are often just part of the backdrop to our daily routines – street trees on our walk to the shops, hedgerow trees flashing by on the commute to work, a clump of trees seen from an office window, eating a sandwich under a tree at lunchtime. Despite the low level of tree cover in Britain, trees populate our private gardens, our shared spaces and our towns and countryside. They frame our open areas and shape the 'spirit of the place'. Look around you and ask yourself what this place would be without trees? What would be lost? Then ask, what would it be like with more trees?

Trees in forests and woods constitute the majority of our national canopy cover, but in our sparsely treed country the trees *outside* woods have a particularly significant role to play: hedgerows, avenues, orchards, solitary trees in fields, trees in farmland, riparian woodland along rivers and streams. All these contribute to our canopy and provide islands of habitat. Trees outside woods cover 3 per cent of all land in the UK, with three quarters of these trees in the countryside and one quarter in towns. Historically, there used to be many more. Trees in hedges and fields and woods both great and small largely define the character of the countryside by their presence or absence. Our history of enclosure by hedgerows has led to an unusually high number of individual trees and hedges in the countryside. Some of these are surviving timber trees and some surviving pollards.

We often think of the trees growing in fields and hedges as 'natural' features, but they are not. Most were deliberately planted and managed, and even if they were not, a conscious decision was often made to allow them to grow. The landscape historian Tom Williamson has found that prior to 1850 the countryside was 'absolutely filled with trees' and these were mostly pollards growing in hedges, such that they

In farmed landscape, with close-set and varied patches of wildlife habitat, hedges shelter, feed and support thousands of different species, including us. Birds, mammals, plants, invertebrates: think of the millions of creatures that rely on hedges for life. If regularly trimmed, hedges become a dense thicket from base to top. Too much trimming deprives the insects of flowers and the birds of berries; too little trimming allows gaps to appear in the hedge. A three-year cycle seems to be the best middle ground for cutting hedges, but it will depend on species, growth and location. Photograph by Nigel Mykura.

appeared as 'one continuous grove'. Although the wider use of coal and the introduction of bigger fields dramatically reduced the numbers of hedgerow pollards, hedges were still intensively managed by farmers for specific purposes, such as producing fodder for animals and poles for hedging and fencing. This purely functional view of trees was part of policy and thinking until the 1947 Town and Country Planning Act introduced Tree Preservation Orders (TPOs), which represented a 'triumph of the new attitude to trees – as objects of the natural world to be preserved, rather than as economic objects to be husbanded and exploited.' After the Second World War, however, about half of our hedges were lost to field expansion, roads, development, Dutch Elm Disease and neglect. It wasn't until 1997 that this loss was slowed by the introduction of the Hedgerow Regulation legislation, but old hedges are still being lost and their replacement with a couple of new rows of hawthorn is just not the same.

In contrast to other northern European countries, hedges remain a key feature of our landscapes, embodying history, habitats for plants and animals and local distinctiveness whilst providing shelter and enclosure. Stretching some 500,000 miles, they are

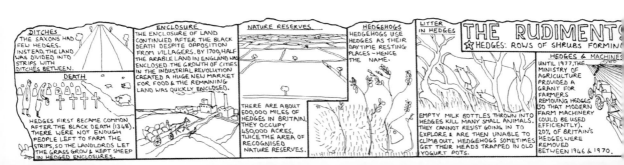

DITCHES
THE SAXONS HAD FEW HEDGES. INSTEAD, THE LAND WAS DIVIDED INTO STRIPS WITH DITCHES BETWEEN.

DEATH
HEDGES FIRST BECAME COMMON AFTER THE BLACK DEATH (1348). THERE WERE NOT ENOUGH PEOPLE LEFT TO FARM THE STRIPS, SO THE LANDLORDS LET THE GRASS GROW & KEPT SHEEP IN HEDGED ENCLOSURES.

ENCLOSURE
THE ENCLOSURE OF LAND CONTINUED AFTER THE BLACK DEATH DESPITE OPPOSITION FROM VILLAGERS. BY 1700, HALF THE ARABLE LAND IN ENGLAND WAS ENCLOSED. THE GROWTH OF CITIES IN THE INDUSTRIAL REVOLUTION CREATED A HUGE NEW MARKET FOR FOOD & THE REMAINING LAND WAS QUICKLY ENCLOSED.

NATURE RESERVES
THERE ARE ABOUT 600,000 MILES OF HEDGES IN BRITAIN. THEY OCCUPY 450,000 ACRES, TWICE THE AREA OF RECOGNISED NATURE RESERVES.

HEDGEHOGS
HEDGEHOGS USE HEDGES AS THEIR DAYTIME RESTING PLACES – HENCE THE NAME.

LITTER IN HEDGES
EMPTY MILK BOTTLES THROWN INTO HEDGES KILL MANY SMALL ANIMALS. THEY CANNOT RESIST GOING IN TO EXPLORE & ARE THEN UNABLE TO CLIMB OUT. HEDGEHOGS SOMETIMES GET THEIR HEADS TRAPPED IN OLD YOGURT POTS.

THE RUDIMENTS
☆ HEDGES: ROWS OF SHRUBS FORMIN[G]

HEDGES & MACHINES
UNTIL 1977, THE MINISTRY OF AGRICULTURE PROVIDED A GRANT FOR FARMERS REMOVING HEDGES SO THAT MODERN FARM MACHINERY COULD BE USED EFFICIENTLY). 20% OF BRITAIN'S HEDGES WERE REMOVED BETWEEN 1946 & 1970.

said to be the largest 'semi-natural' habitat in Britain (they are essentially made by us but sustained by nature). We are extremely lucky to have well-hedged landscapes.

The Campaign to Protect Rural England (CPRE) describes hedgerows as 'the vital stitching in the patchwork quilt of the English countryside'. They can also be seen as the edges where wild nature has survived or pushed up in between the slabs of agriculture. A mature and diverse hedge will provide an avenue of abundance for wildlife in stark contrast to the monoculture of crops either side, enabling plants to flourish and providing wildlife with food and connecting corridors across less sheltered, more inhospitable farmland. Old hedges can take on magnificent and

Trees outside woods help to create our classic rural landscape: hedges, hedgerow trees and copses frame the fields and settlements.

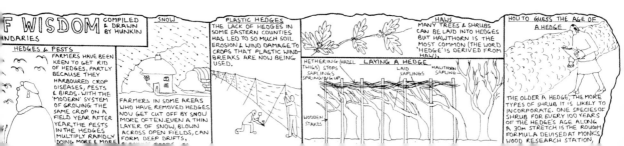

F WISDOM COMPILED & DRAWN BY HUNKIN

NDARIES

HEDGES & PESTS
FARMERS HAVE BEEN KEEN TO GET RID OF HEDGES, PARTLY BECAUSE THEY HARBOURED CROP DISEASES, PESTS & BIRDS, WITH THE 'MODERN' SYSTEM OF GROWING THE SAME CROP ON A FIELD YEAR AFTER YEAR, THE PESTS IN THE HEDGES MULTIPLY RAPIDLY DOING MORE & MORE

SNOW
FARMERS IN SOME AREAS WHO HAVE REMOVED HEDGES NOW GET CUT OFF BY SNOW MORE OFTEN. EVEN A THIN LAYER OF SNOW, BLOWN ACROSS OPEN FIELDS, CAN FORM DEEP DRIFTS,

PLASTIC HEDGES
THE LACK OF HEDGES IN SOME EASTERN COUNTIES HAS LED TO SO MUCH SOIL EROSION & WIND DAMAGE TO CROPS THAT PLASTIC WIND-BREAKS ARE NOW BEING USED.

LAYING A HEDGE
HETHERING (HAZEL TWIGS) STOPS SAPLINGS SPRINGING UP
LAID SAPLINGS
HALTINGS SAPLING
WOODEN STAKES

HAWS
MANY TREES & SHRUBS CAN BE LAID INTO HEDGES BUT HAWTHORN IS THE MOST COMMON (THE WORD 'HEDGE' IS DERIVED FROM HAW).

HOW TO GUESS THE AGE OF A HEDGE
THE OLDER A HEDGE, THE MORE TYPES OF SHRUB IT IS LIKELY TO INCORPORATE. ONE SPECIES OF SHRUB FOR EVERY 100 YEARS OF THE HEDGE'S AGE ALONG A 30m STRETCH IS THE ROUGH FORMULA DEVISED AT MONK'S WOOD RESEARCH STATION,

Hedgerow trees are a distinctive feature of the countryside, but we cannot take them for granted. Elm was a major hedgerow tree that largely disappeared in the 1970s and now ash is in a similar position. Open grown trees in hedges often mature to become ancient trees. Out in the Atlantic, these elms on the Scilly Isles escaped Elm Disease. Photograph by Oliver Rackham, courtesy of Jenny Moody.

wonderful forms, with shapes that express their age and historic role in the landscape.

There has been interest recently in managing hedges for woodfuel by allowing them to grow tall for ten years or so, then coppicing them for firewood and chipwood. This elegant system is widely practised in Brittany and Normandy as *bocage* and could play a role here, too. It is important not to lose all the benefits of our traditional hedges, but for some hedges in some locations it might be appropriate. The most productive species for *bocage*, according to the Devon Hedge Group, are willow, ash, oak, beech and sycamore, all trees which do not make the traditional dense thicket hedge. So if these species are present and machine access is possible, it might be worth considering. As well as the woodfuel, there will be additional benefits of shelter, carbon sequestration and less annual hedge trimming.

Woodland that stretches along the banks of rivers and streams create an edge habitat of great benefit to the aquatic ecosystem. The roots of trees, especially alders, bind the soil to prevent erosion and provide habitat niches along the banks. The canopy casts shade

THE 'PHOENIX' TREE IN THE DICK TURPIN ORCHARD, ESSEX

Dick Turpin orchard is home to several different fruit trees: plum, pear and apple, including a 'phoenix' tree that blew over one winter and has since sent up new shoots. These veteran trees are a wonderful habitat for wildlife, such as the shaggy polypore bracket fungus, where a rare beetle was found that has not been recorded near London since 1928. A group from the community have been restoring and learning about Dick Turpin's trees, with expert help from The Orchard Project. The orchard itself (beside the Dick Turpin pub in Ilford, Essex) is almost 100 years old, and some local residents of Aldborough Hatch, near Newbury Park, have memories of the orchard in its prime. The group is ensuring that the orchard becomes a haven for all the community to enjoy. As well as restoring many other 'lost orchards', The Orchard Project has set up a juice and craft-cider enterprise and is also training adults and children to care for their orchards.

Trees in every landscape can mitigate the worst effects of climate breakdown by absorbing carbon and holding it in wood or underground, affording shelter and shade, and providing an alternative energy source to fossil carbon. Along rivers, trees also reduce the fertiliser or pesticide running off agricultural fields into the water.

to prevent excessive heat and weed growth and falling leaves and insects contribute to the food chain, particularly important in uplands where aquatic vegetation is sparse. The greater the variety of species the better, as leaves decompose at different rates, offering sustained nutrition.

Conifers, however, can cast too much shade on the water and on the ground vegetation. Blocks of upland Sitka spruce were regularly planted across the hillsides without regard to the watercourses, but it is now standard practice when felling and replanting to leave a buffer zone of several metres, often with occasional broadleaved trees, to improve the stream ecology.

In the management of a stream or river, there is the temptation to remove fallen deadwood. It might look tidier to our eyes, but deadwood can slow water flow and create pools, which become more diverse habitats for fish and insects. The few colonies of beavers in Scotland, Yorkshire and Devon seem to be creating these pools, too.

Belts of riparian woodland can also act as buffers between intensively farmed land and watercourses, trapping fertilisers

New planting on the floodplain near Ilminster, Somerset. Trees are an ally in natural flood management. Trees soak up water themselves, improve soil structure and infiltration, and woody material can be used in the form of leaky dams to slow down the flow of water across the landscape. Photograph by Sabine Peukert.

and pesticides before they reach the water. Ecologist George Peterken identifies riparian and floodplain woodland as key areas for expansion – they are ecologically rich, naturally connecting corridors in the landscape and unsuitable for development.

Trees at home

Each patio, balcony and garden is a personal oasis and a living laboratory for forming a relationship with nature. Travelling by train is a wonderful way to glimpse behind the fence and see how we actually live with trees. Some gardens attempt total domination: suppressing grass, flowers, trees and all living things in favour of paving, decking or tarmac for cars. Other gardeners keep trees as pets: tamed and domesticated, pruned like tightly cropped lollipops, while their neighbours might ignore the trees completely or use them as useful posts for hanging a washing-line.

Even on the smallest balcony you can grow a variety of trees in pots, including apples, pears and apricots, so you can create a micro arboretum or orchard. And you don't have to have a large garden to grow trees: birch, rowan, hawthorn and elder are particularly suited to small gardens. All trees will attract wildlife, too: birds, insects and perhaps butterflies and bees

THE CHRISTMAS TREE 1848
The German tradition of a decorated fir tree was introduced to Britain by the Royal Family, as early as the 1790s, but did not become public practice until The London Illustrated News published a woodcut print of the Christmas tree at Windsor Castle in 1848. Within two years it becomes very fashionable to display an evergreen tree festooned with decorations.

A cherry tree in Leeds allowed to grow to full stature.

HORSE CHESTNUT 1600
From its natural range in the Balkans, specimens of this broadleaf tree are brought into England for their amazing blossom, to decorate the parks and gardens of the wealthy

if it's not too high up. If the trees grow too big they could be transplanted into a suitable place in your neighbourhood.

Most people have found a middle way of living with trees that is, more or less, harmonious: a wild cherry becomes a cloud of insect-friendly blossom in spring and fiery shades of red and orange in autumn; an espalier apple tree yields home-grown fruits in the smallest of spaces; a magnificent beech allowed to grow to full stature becomes the roosting place for owls; a trimmed hawthorn hedge shelters nesting birds, insects and other wildlife; fast-growing birch trees soon attract insects and the birds that feed off them; the branches of a laburnum are a place where children can play and explore the furthest reaches of their imagination all year round; yew, holly and ivy provide the birds with winter roosting and food.

Trees are not static, they grow, change, die – and so do people and their houses – so this balance between people and trees is always shifting. Garden trees make a huge contribution to our built landscape – a recent study in London found that 60 per cent of the urban canopy was in private gardens. As well as the benefits of shelter, shade, beauty and habitat, these individual specimens combine to form an urban arboretum of astonishing diversity – cockspur thorns with huge berries and rich autumn colour, many varieties of apple, pear and cherry with glorious spring blossom, Manna ash with frothy flowers, 'Raywood' ash with sunset colours and 'Jaspidea' ash with golden bark.

Edgelands: trees, like wildlife in general, will grab the opportunity for life wherever they can. In Shaftesbury, Dorset, these ash trees push up through the cracks in a recently finished building development, and are more successful than the trees that were planted in the small square patches in the paving on the left (now covered over), which were vandalised and died.

Trees in our streets

Venturing out into the streets, we see that some urban areas are surprisingly well wooded. Just as there is wide variation in woodland cover throughout Britain, there is variation within our towns and cities. Generally, there are more trees in southern towns than northern towns, and coastal towns in particular have fewer trees, often with less than 10 per cent canopy cover.

Jesus Green in Cambridge. Plane trees forming an avenue, defining and enclosing this beautiful public park.

LONDON PLANE
London plane trees are not native to London, nor to the UK. Their precise origins are unknown but most botanists agree they are a hybrid between the Oriental Plane and the American Sycamore (Platanus occidentalis), and more likely a result of early phases of globalisation.

Trees push up through the cracks and edgelands of our towns and cities, just as elsewhere, and can often thrive if we let them. With four out of five of us living in towns and cities, this is where most people will encounter trees and where their many benefits will be most widely felt. As there are fewer trees and more people in towns, each of these brave trees has a proportionally higher 'social value', providing shelter from sun and wind, filtering pollution and bringing little oases of nature to city-dwellers.

Many of the benefits of trees depend on the leaf area of the tree: the bigger the tree, the greater the leaf area, the more shelter, screening and habitat. So it is really important to allow big trees to grow and reach full potential. Rather than replace giant plane trees, for example, with more easily managed cherry trees, we must insist on keeping as many large trees as possible, replacing like for like.

One particular feature of trees that deserves special mention

Red Cross Gardens, Borough, London; a calm and peaceful community garden, opposite a school.

is their role in the carbon cycle. As if trees were not already the most amazing and wonderful living things, they also absorb carbon dioxide from the air and lock it into wood. It's hard to imagine a more useful contribution to life on Earth. Carbon dioxide, water and light are absorbed by trees to make carbohydrates and oxygen by photosynthesis. All green plants perform this process, but the special thing about trees is that their carbohydrates are mostly turned into wood – strong, durable, workable, beautiful.

Trouble with trees

'Surely you're not going to cut it down?'; 'Could you just take that branch off as well because it shades my patio?'; 'Fell the whole tree so I don't have to clear up the leaves!' An arborist,

In January 2015, the Save Southwark Woods campaign was founded in order to protect the Camberwell Cemeteries and their woods, graves, allotments, playing fields and meadows, which the council wants to use for new burial spaces.

TOLPUDDLE
MARTYRS 1834
In 1834 six agricultural
labourers gather under
a Dorset sycamore
tree to form the first
Trade Unions in Britain,
bargaining for better pay
and working conditions.

chainsaw in hand, preparing to prune or fell a tree, is often confronted by the contradictory perspectives and meanings that trees have for people.

Our culture seems to have a love–hate relationship with trees. We romanticise them; our encounters with them are meaningful and valuable in many ways, but we are also disappointed when they don't behave as we wish. We love the blossom but net trees to prevent birds from nesting. We admire the autumn colours until the leaves block our gutters. We hate to see them cut down but need more mobile phone masts. Really, we do love trees, if only they didn't impinge quite so much on our busy lives, lifting paving slabs, undermining foundations, brushing against our cars and homes. Names such as Seven Sisters, Elm Grove or Walnut Tree Walk reflect the local importance of trees, which in some cases were present even before the houses were built. But trees can struggle in urban places. They are often alone in pavements and tarmac with compacted soils, pollutants in the air, searing heat and insufficient water. As the forester and author Peter Wohlleben describes, street trees are 'the street kids of the forest' and lack the support of their families and a 'cosy, calm, moist forest around them.'

The great diversity of trees can improve the resilience of our urban forests, but some species are particularly vulnerable.

The BIG sycamore tree was like a LANDMARK

When I was born in 1982, it already towered high above our late 70s built bungalow in rural county Tyrone. IT was a constant feature of my childhood - I practically grew up under it's branches. Often I worried what would happen if it fell over and landed on our house. What if it got hit by lightning? Would it CRUSH US ALL? My dad's heifers loved to strip it's lowest branches of their leaves.

Sycamore

BY BARRY FALLS

I HAD AT LEAST 3 treehouses at various times in its branches and one time my brother climbed so high up that I felt sick just watching him. We had bonfires beside it every HALLOWE'EN. Lots and lots of swings. It was always there, just a big, beautiful tree. I probably took it for granted, but I did LOVE it.

LAST YEAR, without much warning, it blew over in a storm and that was that. My wife salvaged a few logs from it so her grandfather could turn a couple of bowls from them. We have one at our front door; it holds my car keys and a couple of random bits of lego.

London plane trees outside The Old Vic Theatre on London's South Bank.

Plane trees, for example, play a vital role in London, where their huge size and leaf area provide many benefits. But they are threatened by Plane Wilt, a disease from North America now making its way up through Europe, spread by human activity and planting infected stock.

Extreme weather events are another threat, becoming more frequent with climate change, and trees in towns and cities can have less protection than their cousins in the countryside. And when they shed branches or fall, they can cause more damage, so great vigilance is needed to ensure the health of urban trees. Wind is an obvious cause of damage to trees, but so too is flooding from storm surges in many coastal towns.

SELL THE FOREST! 2010
The coalition government announces plans to sell part of the Public Forest estate in England, including ancient woodland, into private hands. Hundreds of thousands of people object, and in 2011 the government abandons the plan.

In Sheffield, the City Council and a highways maintenance contractor, perhaps thinking they were doing the right things to keep their citizens 'safe', were confronted with protests and anger at the way they decided to deal with 'troublesome' street trees (*see* page 65). In 2019, Reading Borough Council admitted that its maintenance team cut down 800 saplings because they were 'not clearly visible amongst the nettles and brambles'. We can love trees and say we want to care for them, but putting these sentiments and ideas into action, with funding, training and support, is less straightforward. This failure of practice is no

TREE PRESERVATION ORDERS

All types and species of tree can be protected by TPOs, including single trees or groups of trees, hedges and woods. Most trees within a conservation area are also protected.

TPOs are made by the local planning authority (usually a local council) to protect trees from felling, uprooting, topping or any wilful damage. Any works to trees with TPOs require permission from the local authority and consent can be subject to conditions.

Records and maps of TPOs or conservation areas are held by the council planning office and often available online. If you think work is being carried out illegally contact the council tree officer or environment team straight away.

longer good enough. Trees create a sense of place and democracy creates a sense of belonging – both have been undermined by tree strategies that put short-term costs above long-term local benefits.

These direct threats to urban trees could be dismissed as examples of misconduct or mistakes in a few, isolated places. But the threats to trees are systematic when we think about new building developments in towns. The building of every new home, extension, road, hospital, school or industrial area conflicts with wildlife in some way, continuing our age-old suppression of nature. Even if sound environmental plans are submitted in planning stages, they are not necessarily enforceable by councils if a developer decides not to follow it all through. Are there ways we can improve the way we share space with nature?

Any local council – county, town or parish – has a crucial role to play in shaping policies and in planning legislation, such as Tree Preservation Orders (TPOs) and Conservation Areas – although neither guarantees a tree's protection. If people are working on

Netting trees has grown in recent years as a way for developers to prevent birds from nesting. This may be because the tree is about to be felled, or because building works are starting soon, or may even be to protect the birds from these works. It is legal to net trees, but an offence to destroy an active nest. There have been widespread complaints about netting from conservation groups!

THE KINDER SCOUT MASS TRESPASS 1932
A mass trespass is undertaken at Kinder Scout, in the Peak District of Derbyshire, on 24 April. This act of wilful trespass by ramblers highlights the fact that walkers in England and Wales were denied access to areas of open country.

trees in the neighbourhood, you are well within your rights to ask them who has authorised the work and whether they have obtained permission to do it from the landowner or council. Let your feelings be known!

All local authorities *should* have a meaningful Tree Strategy for the care and maintenance of their current trees, a plan for their replacement when necessary, targets for new planting to increase tree cover to 20 per cent, and for new housing to have a minimum of 30 per cent canopy cover (as recommended by the Woodland Trust).

Learning to value trees

In New York City it was estimated that for every $1 invested in the city's trees, there was $5 of public benefit and this made a compelling case for funding. The City Council adopted a strategy of 'block planting', where the default position was to plant trees in streets unless there was a reason not to. They also pursued 'environmental equity' across the city, focusing planting in places with the most people and the least trees, typically the poorer neighbourhoods. But how did they come up with these calculations?

Trees might filter out air pollutants and screen out noise, cool the city in summer by transpiration and slow rainfall and storm run-off, but how do we express the value of these

DEFENDING THE URBAN FOREST

Residents and protesters in Meersbrook Park and Chippinghouse Road in Sheffield expressing their affection for trees and anger in response to the City Council's particularly stark attitude to street trees. Photographs by Pixelwitch and Fran Halsall.

Sheffield looks different from many British cities. Spread across hills and valleys, it sits within a matrix of woodland covering 18.4 per cent of the land, including some 36,000 street trees. As part of the Streets Ahead highways upgrade programme, in 2018 the contractor Amey set about felling 5,500 trees. They even had plans to fell up to half of the city's street trees before they ran into vociferous protests from outraged residents.

The Private Finance Initiative between the City Council and Amey, signed in 2012, is worth £2.1 billion over 25 years. Some suspect Amey of felling trees as a cost-cutting measure, rather than because they are dying, diseased or dangerous.

The matter was made worse by an apparent lack of consultation and because there were alternative solutions to cutting down the trees, according to the council's own Independent Tree Panel.

Protesters from Sheffield Tree Action Group (STAG) have now reached agreement with the council to review the felling plans, as a result of which many trees are to be spared the chop, for now at least.

These Sheffield street trees have raised fundamental questions about the ownership of public assets, and how they are going to be managed for future generations.

i-Tree is software developed by the US Department of Agriculture Forest Service with a range of tools that enables people to carry out a variety of tasks, from recording individual trees on the street to making benefit analysis of urban and rural forests. The i-Tree tools are being used around the world in forest management and advocacy efforts by quantifying forest structure and the many benefits of trees.

natural benefits? And should we put a price on nature at all? We may well agree that trees and woods support health and wellbeing and underpin the economy by improving the quality of workplaces and homes, but unless they appear on a budget spreadsheet these benefits will be ignored. People also like to gather by trees, so a collection of trees in a park, orchard or planted along a street can make all the difference, softening an otherwise hard landscape of tarmac and brick into an avenue of blossom, shade and movement. But can you really account for a web of interactions and emotional relationships? And how do we calculate the food and shelter that trees provide so that wildlife can thrive in our towns and cities?

In the quest for tools to support the case for more trees in our lives, 'ecosystem services' are an attempt to put a monetary value on nature. For example, planting trees upstream in the catchment can slow water flow and prevent expensive flooding downstream, so it is possible to calculate the flood-prevention value of each hectare of woodland, which turns out to be about £100–150 per hectare per year in perpetuity (according to one Woodland Trust study). A recent report on Hyde Park in London concluded that the trees provide 'an amenity asset value of a staggering £173 million'.

The Office of National Statistics estimates that 'the non-market benefits of woodland exceed the market benefits of timber by approximately 12 times; timber represents £275 million out of £3.3 billion total annual value of woodland in 2017.' This means that the average value of the timber at the point of felling was worth about £25 per tonne, but the value of long-term benefits expected from carbon sequestration, recreation, air pollution removal, urban cooling, noise reduction (and many more) is vastly higher. On top of this, there are many unquantifiable values – beauty, habitat, special places, favourite trees – that we can only guess at.

Payment for Ecosystem Services (PES) schemes reward forest owners for the services provided by their trees. The Forestry Commission grant scheme works in this way, paying landowners to manage woods for public benefit.

When the Woodland Trust decided to commission an ecosystem services review of UK's woods, the report *The Economic Benefits*

of Woodland concluded that, with a few qualifications, 'the total value of UK woodlands is around £270 billion'. The report has the admirable aim of drawing attention to the very wide range of benefits brought by trees, so that decisions are made with better understanding. If our woods are worth £270 billion and there are about 65 million of us in the UK, does that mean by some bizarre logic that they are worth £4,154 to each of us?

In recent years, a variety of valuation tools have been developed to help calculate the 'natural capital' of trees. One of these tools – i-Tree – has been used in many towns to quantify the benefits of trees in monetary terms. Back in 2011, a study carried out in Torbay, Devon, by the town council and the NHS Clinical Commissioning Group, explored the links between health and trees in the town. It concluded that the 'structural value' (the cost of having to replace every single tree with an identical tree) was £280 million. This figure grows as trees grow, and falls as they die. Of course, trees also have 'functional values', such as carbon storage (which was calculated as over £5 million) and annual air-pollution removal of ozone, carbon monoxide, nitrogen dioxide, sulphur dioxide and particulates (£1.3 million).

This pioneering Torbay study, carried out by a social enterprise called Treeconomics, cannot and does not capture the emotional and cultural values of trees. But it is a good starting point because it highlights tangible values and helps argue for better care and more spending on trees. Significantly, this survey in Torbay

In 2011 Torbay was one of the first towns in the UK to place a monetary value on the ecosystem services provided by its trees. By filtering pollutants, storing carbon and improving health and wellbeing, the town's trees, it was calculated, stored 98,100 tonnes of carbon and sequestered a further 4,279 tonnes each year. In the UK, i-Tree and the range of tools it provides have become an increasingly popular way for tree groups and local councils to quantify the ecosystem benefits of trees and the urban forest. Photograph courtesy of Treeconomics.

The entire seaside town of Sidmouth, east Devon, has been designated as an arboretum with the objective of protecting and caring for the trees, both public and private, in the Sid Valley. It is the country's first civic arboretum. When an inventory was carried out, it was estimated that the trees removed £720,000 of pollution and reduced water run-off by 215,000 cubic metres in the valley every year. There are also guided arboretum walks and other events in the local community.

was used successfully to argue for an increase in the town's tree budget. Anybody can commission an i-Tree study. Across the UK, from Sidmouth and Bridport to London, Oxford and Manchester, more and more councils – parish, town and district alike – are following Torbay's example.

The journalist Peter Fiennes argues: 'If, for now, we have to live in a world run by accountants, then at least let's make sure they get their sums right.' After all, in a world of perfect accounting, nature should always win because everything we do depends on it. But even current methods fail to include 'externalities' such as air and water pollution, allowing dirty industries to make unjustifiable profits by dumping their waste on society and nature at large. In *Green and Prosperous Land*, the author Dieter Helm suggests: 'Making polluters pay is the single most radical and effective policy that could be adopted, for economic prosperity and for the environment.'

Is it possible to extend our accounting periods beyond the human time frame, to absorb the slow time of trees? Is ecosystem services just trying to force nature into an economic box that suits our spreadsheets rather than engaging our minds in ways we can value without profit and loss?

Trees for Cities works closely with local communities to cultivate lasting change in their neighbourhoods – whether it's revitalising forgotten spaces, creating healthier environments or getting people interested in growing, foraging and eating healthy food. In 2017, along with 35 volunteers, they surveyed 480 trees in Kennington Park and calculated that they were worth £12.3 million, filtering 528,200 litres of water and removing 8 tonnes of carbon from the atmosphere. Photograph courtesy of Trees for Cities.

Valuations of ecosystem services cannot represent the entire value of trees and woods. Trees and woods are just too complex and dynamic. It might be possible to take a fixed snapshot in time, but these values are temporary and cannot encompass the network of present, past and future life that any one tree sustains. It is like valuing a human being by the money they earn, or their A-levels, or their shoe size. Some of the things people do can be translated into economic value – paid work being the most obvious. But our value as people encompasses much more – as friends, parents, family members, neighbours.

The journalist and activist George Monbiot describes ecosystem services as 'the Natural Capital Agenda: the pricing, valuation, monetisation, financialisation of nature in the name of saving it.' He objects on several grounds: the values are non-commensurable, so you cannot put a price on rarity or beauty; it does not address the disproportionate power in the hands of those who see nature only as a resource for profit; it allows the conservation of the natural world to be framed as an economic calculation of quantities, rather than as an argument about intrinsic values of people and the natural world. Nature is seen merely as a service provider; no longer a slave, but still a servant of humanity.

But the environmental campaigner Tony Juniper questions the idea that nature is a barrier to economic progress. He argues that nature is providing innumerable services to our economy, and measuring it is better than doing nothing.

Perhaps the economic system cannot be revolutionised overnight, so establishing a value for 'services' is a language that is more likely to fund the protection and expansion of tree and woods. The National Forest, for example, is estimated to have brought economic benefits: 2.6 times greater than its investment in the first 20 years, with an anticipated increase to 4.8 times the investment this century.

Professor Adrian Newton and others at Bournemouth University have demonstrated how investing in natural capital and semi-natural ecosystems can improve the local economy and create jobs. Investment could include developing ecological networks, planting woods, creating wetland and grassland, making provisions for rewilding. They argue that it makes more sense to provide incentives for farmers to produce 'public goods' and ecosystem services than increased agricultural yields.

So how do we learn to appreciate the many contributions made by trees and woods, whilst avoiding the dangers of 'the market'? Can the ecosystem services approach help convince people that trees and woods really are valuable and deserve protection?

We need robust protection for the things we value, then there will simply be no contest between an ancient wood and a car park, any more than we would think of demolishing a cathedral for a bypass. But we don't have that yet. Ancient woods are under threat, street trees are cut down when they don't need to be. So we need to assess the worthiness of actions and projects the other way round. Instead of asking what benefit does nature give us, shouldn't we be asking what benefit our plans have for nature?

The time has surely come for us to change our approach and view nature as the primary sustainer of life, and act to support and restore that in all our actions. Social and economic

Flat Iron Square, Borough, London. Plane trees create an island of delight in the dense urban environment. A London-wide report, carried out in 2015 with the aid of volunteers, found that it is the larger trees on public land, in parks and streets, that contribute the most measurable value. Big trees make the biggest difference!

considerations will still be part of the analysis, but will have to work within the discipline of nature. Trees and woods are deeply embedded in our economic life, but they are not just another tradeable commodity – they need appropriate protection within an economic system driven by life-sustaining values.

The urban forest

Trees and woods remain a central part of any green infrastructure, and the conservation of existing trees and promotion of new trees and woods should be integral to the built environment. Unfortunately, the impact of funding cuts turns our relationship with trees into a defensive or reactive one, a liability and a drain on the budget. Although many trees in towns grow as individuals – an array of different species spread across many different owners – when considered together they combine to form the urban forest, both an abstract and real place that offers millions of people better public health, shelter from climate change, social equity, civic pride and contact with nature.

The government has supported the urban forest idea by announcing an Urban Tree Challenge Fund of £10 million match-funding towards the planting of 130,000 trees in England's

The One Tree Per Child project was launched by Bristol City Council in February 2015 with the aim of planting one tree for each of the 36,000 primary school children in Bristol at the time. The project continues to plant at least 6,000 trees in the city every year, one tree for every child starting school. With the help of Bristol's children and their primary schools, as well as environmental partners, community groups and volunteers, the project has planted over 60,000 trees. Photograph by Chris Bahn.

towns and cities. The Urban Forestry and Woodlands Advisory Committee argues that the urban forest vision 'will be shared by developers, planning authorities and communities as a critically important element of plans for new investment, infrastructure and retrofit.' But with so much of the urban forest on private land, joined-up management can become difficult. Greater awareness and education amongst landowners can help shape a more collaborative management approach, but local authorities or organisations able to engage in landscape-scale planning, must inspire new opportunities for communities and wildlife to thrive side by side.

There are different ways for organisations and individuals to play their part in nurturing this urban forest. School grounds, for example, provide excellent opportunities for trees, improving and enriching the surroundings whilst providing a valuable resource for learning on the doorstep. School playing fields and playgrounds are all too often flat and treeless expanses of grass or tarmac. This needn't be so. Look again with trees in mind! While keeping areas open for communal activities and organised games, there are always boundaries and edges. Why not replace unattractive fencing with hedges to soften the appearance and

attract wildlife? As they do in Bristol, you could plant a tree for every new child that starts school, either in the school grounds or somewhere in the local community.

Town parks can be a haven for wildlife and people. Yet they can also be monotonous, over-tidy or places that people completely avoid. By involving nearby residents' associations, businesses or youth clubs in the maintenance of parks, a sense of pride and care can ripple out and increase the number of people using the park. This is what happened as the residents of Wenlock Barn in London took control of a neglected space near their flats. More diversity in *who* cares for communal green spaces brings more variety in *how* they are maintained. The more that people and wildlife are given the chance to express themselves, the more resilient and biodiverse urban forests will become.

Because orchards are a curious cultural hybrid, consisting of naturally growing trees heavily influenced by the interventions

Malls Mire is an area of mixed woodland and wetland habitat situated between Toryglen and Rutherglen in Glasgow Southside. People from the surrounding communities have been working with Urban Roots, a local environmental charity, to manage the woodland since 2009 and improve the biodiversity and access for city-dwellers. Malls Mire was the first Community Woodland in Glasgow and was made a Local Nature Reserve in 2015.

of people, they are an ideal way to expand the urban forest and bring communities together. The idea of Community Orchards is simple: to protect, plant and renew orchards and the associated wildlife within a community organisation. Some orchards have been in public ownership or use for years. In other cases, parish councils, housing associations, residents' groups, schools, eco-groups, youth centres, businesses, art galleries, heritage associations or 'Millennium Greens' have discovered ways for community ownership and meaningful participation.

There are also more opportunities for community groups to get involved with small woods on the edges of towns or the wooded pockets scattered through larger cities like Glasgow, London, Bristol or Leeds. Whether out of austerity or environmental concerns, there has been a growth in small-scale initiatives: firewood groups, education projects and woodland management run by local people for local benefit – genuine community woods. Working in a community wood – cutting firewood or making beanpoles, clearing brambles, running regular art classes, wellbeing walks or even an annual music festival – gives people a reason to visit the woods. Community woods find a balanced way of working with woods, and integrating them into our lives, making specialist knowledge common knowledge, and giving us a chance to take collective responsibility for a piece of our neighbourhood.

Local distinctiveness

Some of the most locally distinctive features in our landscape are not woods but individual trees or groups of trees. From commemorative planted trees, to picturesque clumps, to formal avenues, to gnarled old parish-boundary marker trees, our countryside is punctuated by trees – literally forming the syntax of our landscape. They attract our attention, cause us to remember, draw the eye, make places special. And not only in the countryside – our towns are similarly studded with feature trees. Whilst the rows of limes or flowering cherries can make streets look blandly similar, the right tree in the right place can create a beautiful oasis amongst the buildings.

Our native trees mostly have broad and overlapping natural

A CITY OASIS

On the Wenlock Barn Estate in Hackney, London, a short walk away from the bustling Old Street roundabout, there's a new orchard growing. It was planted in 2012 by a resident group at the estate, called The Growing Kitchen, who have an ongoing gardening project.

Before it was an orchard, the space was used by contractors to store heavy machinery, which led to compacted soil and very low wildlife diversity. But after The Orchard Project came along to help assess its suitability for fruit trees, The Growing Kitchen knocked on doors and leafleted other residents of the estate, inviting them to an orchard design session. A planting date was set and five residents attended 'Orchard Leader Training' to learn about the care of the trees and what it meant to be key volunteers.

Then, one cold winter day in 2012, lots of residents arrived to plant fruit trees, including eating and cooking apples, pears, plums and a medlar. The group then applied for free bulbs from the Metropolitan Park and Garden Association and planted hundreds of daffodils on the site and two more fruit trees in 2014, with a crab apple and apricot added a couple of years later, gifted from Hackney Tree Nursery. Native hedging from the Woodland Trust was then planted around the perimeter of the site and a wildflower meadow with seed from The National Lottery and Kew 'Grow Wild' project was planted.

Gradually, the wildlife started to come back and today the orchard boasts grasshoppers, various bees, butterflies, hoverflies, beetles, goldfinches, blackbirds, blue tits, great tits, sparrows and even the exciting discovery of a carder bee nest.

Passers-by always comment on how beautiful the site is: a true oasis in the heart of the city, whilst residents are proud of what they have done, and feel the calm the orchard gives them in the middle of the city. One older resident says he hasn't seen so many butterflies since the site was bombed in the Second World War. Another resident and orchard volunteer says it 'feels like a little miracle and gives me hope.'

THE ORCHARD PROJECT: theorchardproject.org.uk
WENLOCK BARN AND THE GROWING KITCHEN: wenlockbarntmo.co.uk

A wych elm in Ramsbury, Wiltshire. The naturalist and author Peter Marren recalls: 'Villagers would sit beneath the comforting security of its boughs, gossip and watch the world go by. Children knew the tree from the inside, every crevice and hold, the mattress of dry leaves at its base (useful if you slipped) and the smell of mould and sawdust.' The Ramsbury Elm died in 1983, and was replaced by a maiden oak tree excavated from the earth of Epping Forest.

ranges, but it is possible to associate some trees with certain parts of the country, as described in Common Ground's *England in Particular* by Sue Clifford and Angela King:

> Oaks are our most common woodland trees; sessile oak predominates in the North and West uplands and pedunculate oak in the South and East ... Ash seeks out the limestones, from the Mendips in Somerset to the magnesian limestone in County Durham. Beech prefers chalk downs and wolds and the oolitic limestone of the Cotswolds ... Hornbeam is most comfortable in the Home Counties, and sweet chestnut sticks to the South on acid soils. Alder enjoys plashy places; it still dominates the Broads and wet parts of Breckland in Norfolk and, together with willow, borders the Cheshire meres. Wych elm makes for mixed woodland, especially in the North. Lime woods are found in Lincolnshire, but rarely elsewhere.

On the other hand, some of our native trees have extremely limited ranges, only growing in certain remote gorges. The whitebeams (*Sorbus* species) seem to specialise in this, with distinct species clinging to cliffs in the Avon Gorge and the sea-cliffs in South Glamorganshire.

Another major influence on woodland distribution is local culture and industry. For example, the hornbeam coppices of Essex allude not only to the soil type, but also to the centuries

SEVEN SISTERS TREE MAP, London

The artist Rose de Borman created a community tree map to celebrate the Tottenham neighbourhood in London where she lives. On it she has marked the special and important trees growing in her neighbourhood, including the nearby Seven Sisters, named after seven elms planted around a walnut tree on common land. Rose's wonderful map shows that even in densely populated cities, the history and lives of trees and people are entwined. What would a map of the trees in your community look like? And what stories would they tell? What memories do you and your neighbours have of distinctive local trees? Do any have names or histories – Gospel Oaks, Boundary Oaks, Kissing Trees or Wishing Trees? What would you put on the map?

'I wasn't quite a dendrite when I was a kid, but the laburnum tree at the far end of our little back garden in Birmingham was known as *my tree* for as long as I can remember.' Writer Zaffar Kunial (*pictured here as a boy*) based much of his debut poetry collection, *Us*, on the green spaces around the city and suburbs of Moseley, Birmingham, where he grew up. 'The memories that seem to hold me most are in green pockets, in gardens, parks, bits of woodland.' Photogrpah courtesty of Zaffar Kunial.

of management for firewood and charcoal; the beechwoods of the Chilterns similarly indicate a suitable soil and an industrial heritage of furniture-making; along the North Devon coast are the characteristic sessile-oak coppice woodlands that once served the tanbark and charcoal trades.

The opposite of locally distinctive woods must be the monocultural plantation, the universally generic 'cellulose factory' plonked down with little regard to landscape or local character. They speak of cheap land, low fertility and investment opportunities.

Diseases have eroded some of our local distinctiveness. The billowing English elms that once studded the lowland landscape of England are now only found in memory, in historic landscape paintings, or on the Scilly Isles. Ash dieback looks set to subtract another ubiquitous tree from our uplands and hedgerows. Perhaps the few resilient ash will attain mythic status as 'The Survivors'.

Your local trees

Trees and woods are rarely private, in the sense that they are usually visible to the general public and therefore part of the social space. They belong to the neighbourhood as much as to the notional owner.

Trees are also social beings. They are joined to each other

through a web of connections underground, and they are joined to the wider society of wildlife through countless interactions with bugs, birds and bats above the ground. They are also joined to us in an invisible exchange of carbon dioxide and oxygen, by their moderation of humidity, temperature and pollutants, and by showering the air we breath with feel-good ions and volatile oils.

A good way of exploring these different meanings in your community is by mapping trees or recording stories about them, which Common Ground did during the Exeter Tree Tales project in 2016. This is a good project for a school, parish council, tree group, history society, local museum, or any other social group concerned with the community and its surroundings. Many councils have declared a climate

It's not only ancient or historic trees that matter: peoples' memories of and associations with trees are important, too. In 2016, Common Ground initiated the Tree Tales project to capture the 'labyrinth of stories and memories' in Exeter. A chestnut tree (*above*) planted by Niel Svendsen in a bomb crater has become a war memorial for his brother killed in the Second World War.

emergency, and developing a Tree Plan for your town can be a helpful contribution to addressing this. It gives the council, who probably have some land and some budget, a tangible practical project to work on. The i-Tree tools (*see* pages 66–67) support Tree Plans because they can establish a tree inventory of what's already growing, and attach an economic value to the services these trees have – this is the sort of language budget-squeezed councils and councillors will understand!

Any initiative for trees should start with an assessment of what is already there. Look closely at your local trees and ask yourself: what species do you see, what's under threat, what's missing? Are there lots of trees and woods, or only a few scattered trees? Or are there already too many? Surely not! Are the trees young or old, big or small, healthy or moribund? Are there any particularly special trees, such as ancient hollow hulks, rare species, historical trees? People will have their favourite trees – where are they and what makes them special? All members of the group and beyond can contribute to this. Where are your nearest woods and are they open to the public? Are they neglected, well used, over-used? Are they actively managed, and if so, for what?

SHAFTESBURY
A walk among our trees

MEET THE NEIGHBOURS

In Shaftesbury, Dorset, there is an active Tree Group, formed in 2002 in response to the felling of a fine old sycamore tree – the tree had been wrongly condemned and local people decided that they as citizens should try to ensure that the town trees thrived. Today, the aim of Shaftesbury Tree Group is to enrich tree cover, building community knowledge and responsibility along the way.

Alongside safeguarding individual trees with Tree Preservation Orders and commenting on applications to cut and prune trees, the group organises tree walks and has published two Tree Walk maps. These social activities bring people face-to-face with the town trees and help to widen appreciation of how trees are contributing to town life and enriching the local ecology and landscape. More recently, the Tree Group has been working with the town council on a Shaftesbury Town Tree Plan, nominating areas for planting owned by the council and campaigning for trees to be part of any new housing developments.

These discussions have also led to the involvement of local schools, which often have access to open spaces for growing trees or starting community-tree nurseries. And while tree planting is important to the town, the Tree Group also wants to grow peoples' aspiration to take care of existing trees and ensure the survival, watering and aftercare of trees newly established across the town lands.

Photograph by Paul Harrison

GROW YOUR OWN

Inspired by the Scottish charity Trees for Life, Moor Trees has planted over 100,000 broadleaved trees across Dartmoor and south Devon since it was started in 1997.

Volunteers from nearby villages and towns collaborate with Moor Trees by collecting cuttings or seeds in the late summer and autumn from local woodland and hedgerows which are then nurtured and germinated in seed trays and cold frames in community-tree nurseries. Here the young trees are grown for up to three years before they are ready to be lifted out and planted in native woodland projects and future forests.

Collecting local seed is a good way of conserving local genotypes, which is likely to lead to the growth of saplings that are better adapted to soils and other environmental conditions of the area. It also enables the local communities and individual volunteers to play their part in replanting and restoring the landscape, creating a stronger connection between trees and people.

Moor Trees started to develop the community-tree-nursery idea in 1999 when the first acorns

were collected and sown at Broadley Farm (near Totnes) and Grimstone Manor (near Horrabridge). Over the years, they have fine-tuned their growing techniques: when to collect seed, from which woods and which species. They learnt how each tree species' seed had a certain way it needed to be processed and planted, from whether or not to remove the husk and fleshy pod to stratifying seeds in a fridge or simply leaving them in a bucket of sand and vermiculite all winter, and how to protect against predation from voles and grey squirrels.

From these nurseries Moor Trees planted 2.91 hectares at Scorriton Down, which subsequently led to the expansion of the tree nursery idea into spare allotments, volunteers' gardens and even programmes at HMP Dartmoor. Today, the charity has two tree nurseries growing 25,000 trees a year to supply the 10 hectares of new woodland planted every year.

Moor Trees's ambition is to be self-financing, grow 100,000 trees a year from seed and help plant 100 hectares of new woodland and miles of hedgerows. It also wants to deliver training and provide an advisory service to community-tree nurseries around the UK.

It is important to consider the threats to existing trees and woods. These can range from private homeowners felling trees in their gardens, to landowners selling land for development, to councils planning new roads. What plans are in the pipeline and how might they affect trees and woods? Your local trees may already be protected by a Conservation Area or by Tree Preservation Orders (TPOs). It might be useful for your group to have a tree expert, arborist or forester, and someone familiar with the planning process. This is particularly helpful when considering the Neighbourhood Plan and ensuring that trees and woods are included. Trees must be protected during new developments and there may be some 'planning gain' in the form of tree planting.

If we are aiming for an ecologically connected landscape, how might trees and other natural habitats (meadows, ponds, hedges) help to build this? Are trees a part of any new development? How might those scattered copses be joined up? Would that neglected wood benefit from some intervention, or could a path be opened up for walkers? How might your local forestry operation yield more benefits to the local community? Is there a community orchard? Could you plant a community wood for future generations? Or start a community tree nursery to be sure of the provenance of seedlings? How well prepared is your neighbourhood for climate change? Combining these ideas and exploring your locality, it is exciting to imagine a vision of how more trees and woods could contribute to the place where you live.

MAY IN MAY. FESTOONED WITH A GLARE, GLOWING IN A GALE by Kurt Jackson, St Just, Cornwall, 2017, mixed media on wood panel

Common Ground commissioned the artist Kurt Jackson to return to the same hawthorn tree growing in a hedge near his home at St Just, Penwith, in Cornwall, and respond to how it changed through the seasons. The solitary tree is the remnant of an ancient hedge, and its form has been shaped by the weather and landscape over the years, contorted by wind, nibbled at by sheep and deer.

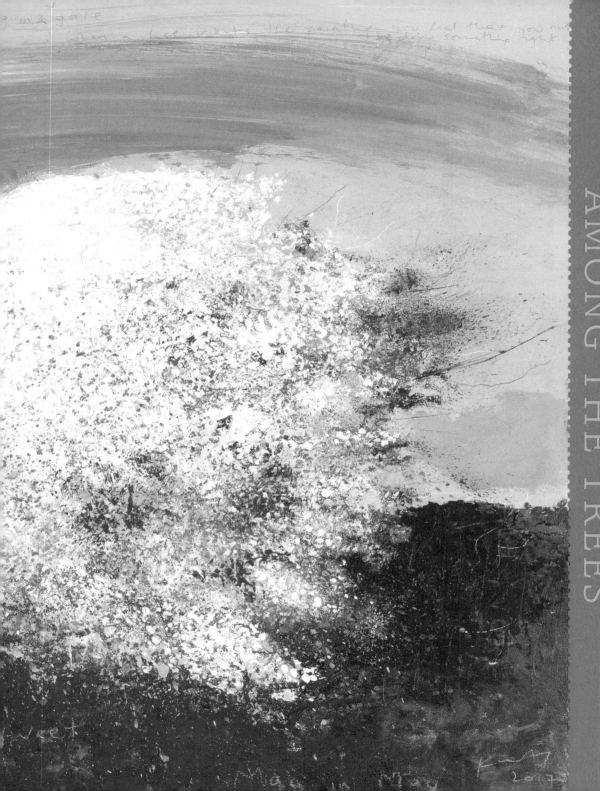

2017

AMONG THE TREES

50 TREES, photographed by Martin Mayer on Waterloo Bridge, London, 1989

Much of Common Ground's past and present work explores the enduring relationship between trees, woods and people. This interest in all things arboreal began in 1986, when the Trees, Woods and the Green Man project invited different artists, photographers, illustrators, poets, cartoonists and writers to explore the natural and cultural value of trees. There were a number of major touring exhibitions of this work, several books and a host of pamphlets, posters, newspapers and postcards. The Tree of Life was an exhibition of painting, photography and sculpture that explored the tree as an archetypal symbol for different cultures all around the world at the Royal Festival Hall (24 July–28 August 1989).

E dward Thomas's poem 'First Known When Lost' recalls a familiar experience:

> I never had noticed it until
> 'Twas gone, – the narrow copse
> Where now the woodman lops
> The last of the willows with his bill.

We *feel* the absence of trees. Edward Thomas felt it at the beginning of the twentieth century, expressing in poetry similar emotions to those felt by people in twenty-first-century Sheffield, who penned songs and prayers and poems to describe their affection for trees like Vernon. It can be shocking each time a tree is *not* encountered, and when we experience this loss or maltreatment on a nearby street or in a local park, the anger and grief we feel tells us something important: if we notice the trees in our lives – at work, in our gardens, in the school grounds, in parks or in streets – we then care about them and are more willing to stand up for them when they are under threat.

In 2011, when the idea of selling off large parts of the state's forest holdings (that's the Forestry Commission woods) was floated in parliament, the prospect of losing 'our' woods created such a public backlash that the Conservative–Liberal Democrat coalition government abandoned the plans. Instead an independent enquiry was commissioned, led by the Bishop of Liverpool, who began with a simple question: 'What do forests and woods mean to you?'

About half of the responses cited what might loosely be called 'social values': access to woods, recreation, health, education, landscape beauty. A further 31 per cent said it was the environmental and wildlife aspects of the wood they valued: the

VIKING BRITAIN 793 AD
Yggdrasil (the World
Tree or Tree of Life)
plays a prominent role in
Norse mythology, which
travelled to the British
Isles with the Viking
invasions, connecting
the existing Romano-
British culture with Norse
cosmology. The branches
of this ash tree extend
into the heavens.

ecological processes, wildlife and nature. Less than 8 per cent mentioned 'economic benefits'.

The pressure group 38 Degrees, which organised an online petition against the proposed sell-off of public forests, analysed their own members' demands and found that they were concerned with three things: that the forests remain in public ownership; that wildlife be protected; and that access be protected. Then, in 2012, the Royal Institute of Chartered Surveyors asked woodland owners how they viewed their woods: the main objective in owning agricultural land was to generate income, but interestingly the main reason for owning woods was for personal pleasure, followed by landscape conservation and biodiversity. The British Woodland Survey of 2017 echoes these findings: 'Protecting/improving nature or biological diversity' was ranked as the most important aim for woodland owners, with 92 per cent of all respondents described as having a 'pro-ecological world view'.

The Forestry Commission also conducts its own 'customer surveys', called the 'Public Opinion of Forestry'. Recent surveys confirm these findings: we see forests as places to relax, enjoy ourselves, keep fit, think, play, have picnics, walk the dog and enjoy wildlife. Significantly, none of these Forestry Commission surveys ranked the forest's contribution to the local economy very highly. Indeed, in the answers to these surveys, the general public and woodland owners appear to see forests and woods as places contributing to our quality of life and that of the natural world, but not as places of economic activity or value.

We seem to have a rather passive relationship with our woods and forests: they are places to go and do something else in, pleasant surroundings for leisure. But we still react strongly to any threat of losing 'our' woods and access to them.

Trees in art

Trees and woods have been loved and venerated in cultures across the world since earliest times, and continue to be a source of inspiration. Of all nature's flora, trees are perhaps the most like people, except they outgrow and outlive us. We hug them, stand among them, admire them. Trees have limbs

THE MAGIC APPLE TREE by Samuel Palmer, 1830

As the largest plant on earth, the tree, an eternal mystical emblem, has been a major source of inspiration for myth and imagination. Trees symbolise longevity, strength and pride. Tree cults, in which a single tree or a grove of trees is worshipped, have flourished at different times almost everywhere. A strong strand of English landscape painting derives from the mystic Arcadia of Celtic and Christian pantheism, which treats the pastoral landscape as a nostalgic, golden age. This idyllic view celebrates abundance in nature: fruit-laden trees, the great oak tree as heart of England. *The Magic Apple Tree* is a watercolour that Samuel Palmer made in 1830, during his 'Visionary' period (c.1826–32), an intense and innovative phase of the artist's life when he painted the landscapes around Shoreham in Kent. Courtesy of Fitzwilliam Museum, University of Cambridge and Bridgeman Images.

and people have dendrites (the branch-like parts of our nervous system that derive their name from *déndron*, Ancient Greek for tree). They even have human-like features: they bleed, wrinkle with age, lose limbs, heal wounds, strive to live on, regardless. Although they are wild and autonomous creatures, perhaps we cannot help but see ourselves in trees, and discover in the woods our different, contradictory human emotions.

Think of the tree's form: stretching from the depths of the earth to the skies above, a strong central stem dividing into boughs, then into branches and twigs, each tree shape defined uniquely by the time and place of its growing. No wonder trees have been a focus for worship and ritual through the ages, and perhaps artistic veneration is a continuation of this reverence and respect for the complexity of life trees communicate to us. Trees and woods are meaningful in so many ways, and it is impossible for us to stop reworking and reshaping them in our arts.

Perhaps one of the reasons that artists are fascinated by trees is because they are so difficult to capture. 'No painting, drawing or photograph,' argued Oliver Rackham, 'can be naturalistic: life isn't long enough to paint all the details.' Although any attempt to describe trees in art will omit more than it includes, there are however some particularly interesting art projects that respond

Trees are central to the work of the acclaimed artist Giuseppe Penone. 'The tree is a spectacular creation because each part of the tree is necessary to its life. It is the perfect sculpture.' Photograph courtesy of the Whitechapel Gallery.

TO DRAW IN THE FOOTSTEPS OF GHOSTS by Christine Mackey, 2017

Christine Mackey is based at the Leitrim Sculpture Centre in Ireland and works across a range of practices and places on projects, public engagements, publications and exhibitions that are meticulously researched. In 2017–18 she was commissioned by Common Ground and the Woodland Trust to explore the relationship that communities in Belfast have with 'millennium woods' (planted as part of the Woods On Your Doorstep millennium programme), so she took to walking them, and along the way collected stories, visited archives and met people who lived and worked near the woods. Christine decided to turn her gaze on wooden benches in the woods, places where people sat and enjoyed the view. She began collecting wood from the different tree species growing near various benches and with these made charcoal with people living in the area. Back in her studio, Christine later used the charcoal to create a wonderful series of ghostly tracings that capture on paper both the sites and trees from which the charcoal was made.

THE
ART
OF THE TREE
AN ARBOREAL MAP
OF THE BRITISH ISLES

DRAWN BY
ADAM DANT
2017

TREE TRAILS traces a 200-year-old story of trees in British art, celebrating the cultural history we share with our arboreal neighbours. It is an invitation to explore this rich seam of wood culture wherever you might live.

The artworks featured on the map are either on permanent display or in national collections across Wales, Scotland, England and Ireland. Trees and woods are both the frame within which the human drama unfolds and the material of choice for the artwork itself.

Celebrating the 80th anniversary of the Charter of the Forest, *Tree Trails* was created for the Woodland Trust by Common Ground and illustrated by Adam Dant.

Charter
for Trees, Woods
and People

COMMON GROUND

WOODLAND
TRUST

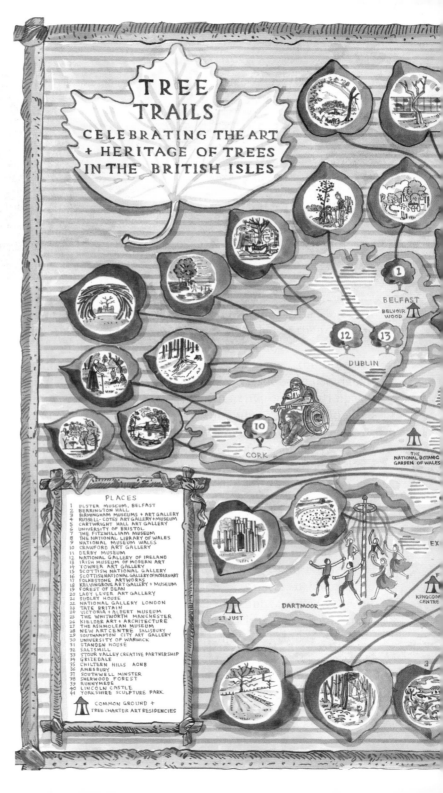

TREE
TRAILS
CELEBRATING THE ART
+ HERITAGE OF TREES
IN THE BRITISH ISLES

PLACES

1 ULSTER MUSEUM, BELFAST
2 BERRINGTON HALL
3 BIRMINGHAM MUSEUMS + ART GALLERY
4 RUSSELL-COTES ART GALLERY + MUSEUM
5 CARTWRIGHT HALL ART GALLERY
6 UNIVERSITY OF BRISTOL
7 THE FITZWILLIAM MUSEUM
8 THE NATIONAL LIBRARY OF WALES
9 NATIONAL MUSEUM WALES
10 CRAWFORD ART GALLERY
11 DERBY MUSEUM
12 NATIONAL GALLERY OF IRELAND
13 IRISH MUSEUM OF MODERN ART
14 TOWNER ART GALLERY
15 SCOTTISH NATIONAL GALLERY
16 SCOTTISH NATIONAL GALLERY OF MODERN ART
17 FOLKESTONE ARTWORKS
18 KELVINGROVE ART GALLERY + MUSEUM
19 FOREST OF DEAN
20 LADY LEVER ART GALLERY
21 SUDLEY HOUSE
22 NATIONAL GALLERY LONDON
23 TATE BRITAIN
24 VICTORIA + ALBERT MUSEUM
25 THE WHITWORTH MANCHESTER
26 KIELDER ARTS + ARCHITECTURE
27 THE ASHMOLEAN MUSEUM
28 NEW ART CENTRE SALISBURY
29 SOUTHAMPTON CITY ART GALLERY
30 UNIVERSITY OF WARWICK
31 STANDEN HOUSE
32 SALTSMILL
33 STOUR VALLEY CREATIVE PARTNERSHIP
34 GRIZEDALE
35 CHILTERN HILLS AONB
36 AMESBURY
37 SOUTHWELL MINSTER
38 SHERWOOD FOREST
39 RUNNYMEDE
40 LINCOLN CASTLE
41 YORKSHIRE SCULPTURE PARK

⛩ COMMON GROUND +
TREE CHARTER ART RESIDENCIES

BELFAST
BELVOIR WOOD
1
12
13
DUBLIN
10
CORK
THE NATIONAL BOTANIC GARDEN OF WALES
EX
F
KINGCOM
CENTRE
ST JUST
DARTMOOR
3

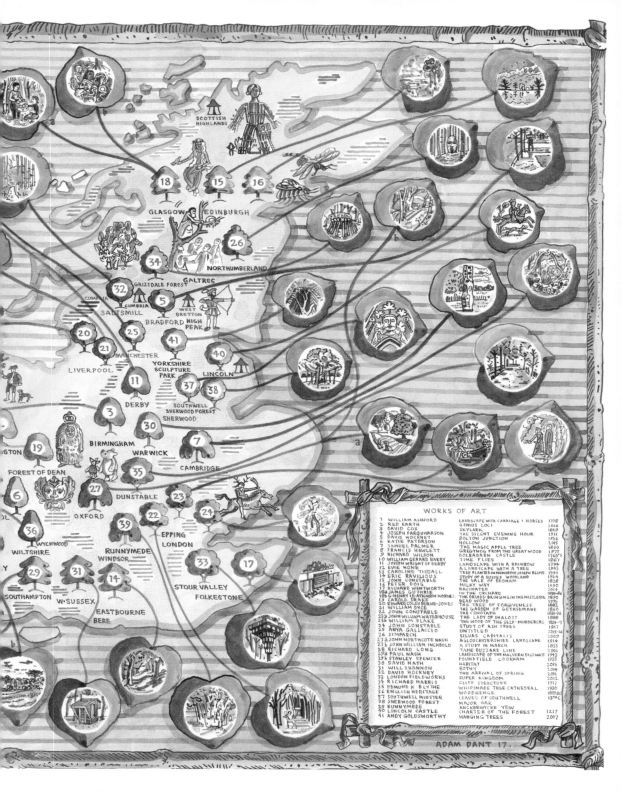

WORKS OF ART

1	WILLIAM ASHFORD	LANDSCAPE WITH CARRIAGE & HORSES	1778
2	RED EARTH	GENIUS LOCI	2016
3	DAVID COX	SKYLARK	1849
4	JOSEPH FARQUHARSON	THE SILENT EVENING HOUR	1911
5	DAVID HOCKNEY	BOLTON JUNCTION	1956
6	KATIE PATERSON	HOLLOW	2015
7	SAMUEL PALMER	THE MAGIC APPLE TREE	1830
8	FRANCIS HEWLETT	GREGYNOG FROM THE GREAT WOOD	1977
9	RICHARD WILSON	DOLBADARN CASTLE	1760'S
10	WILLIAM GERARD BARRY	TIME FLIES	1887
11	JOSEPH WRIGHT OF DERBY	LANDSCAPE WITH A RAINBOW	1794
12	EVIE HONE	A LANDSCAPE WITH A TREE	1945
13	CAROLINE TISDALL	TREE PLANTED IN MEMORY OF JOSEPH BEUYS	1991
14	ERIC RAVILIOUS	STUDY OF A SUSSEX WOODLAND	1934
15	JOHN CONSTABLE	THE VALE OF BEDHAM	1828
16	PETER DOIG	MILKY WAY	1990
17	RICHARD WENTWORTH	RACINATED	2019
18a	JAMES GUTHRIE	IN THE ORCHARD	1885-86
18b	G. HENRY & E.ATKINSON HORNEL	THE DRUIDS-BRINGING IN THE MISTLETOE	1890
19	CAROLE DRAKE	DEAD WOOD	1995
20	EDWARD COLEY BURNE-JONES	THE TREE OF FORGIVENESS	1882
21	WILLIAM DYCE	THE GARDEN OF GETHSEMANE	1860
22	JOHN CONSTABLE	THE CENOTAPH	1833-36
23a	JOHN WILLIAM WATERHOUSE	THE LADY OF SHALOTT	1888
23b	WILLIAM BLAKE	THE WOOD OF THE SELF-MURDERERS	1824-7
24	JOHN CONSTABLE	STUDY OF ASH TREES	1817
25	ANYA GALLACCIO	UNTITLED	2015-16
26	SIMPACH	SILVA'S CAPITALIS	2009
27a	JOHN NORTHCOTE NASH	A GLOUCESTERSHIRE LANDSCAPE	1914
27b	JOHN WILLIAM INCHBOLD	A STUDY IN MARCH	1855
28	RICHARD LONG	TAME BUZZARD LINE	2001
29a	PAUL NASH	LANDSCAPE OF THE MALVERN DISTANCE	1943
29b	STANLEY SPENCER	POUNDFIELD COOKHAM	1915
30	DAVID NASH	HABITAT	2015
31	WILL SHANNON	BOTHY	2014
32	DAVID HOCKNEY	THE ARRIVAL OF SPRING	2011
33	LONDON FIELDWORKS	SUPER KINGDOM	2012
34	RICHARD HARRIS	CLIFF STRUCTURE	1977
35	EDMUND B. BLYTHE	WHIPSNADE TREE CATHEDRAL	1930
36	ENGLISH HERITAGE	WOODHENGE	1800BC
37	SOUTHWELL MINSTER	LEAVES OF SOUTHWELL	13TH C.
38	SHERWOOD FOREST	MAJOR OAK	
39	RUNNYMEDE	ANCKERWYCKE YEW	
40	LINCOLN CASTLE	CHARTER OF THE FOREST	1217
41	ANDY GOLDSWORTHY	HANGING TREES	2007

ADAM DANT 17.

For Ellie Davies forests are 'potent symbols in folklore, fairytale and myth, places of enchantment and magic, as well as of danger and mystery'. They are also ideal places for to create her 'altered' images, such as 'The Dwellings 2' (*above*), which explore the relationship between the landscape and the individual.

to current issues and concerns.

The Woodland Trust and Common Ground collaborated on a series of artist residencies across England, Wales, Scotland and Northern Ireland. In 2017–18, eight artists responded to the 800th anniversary of the Charter of the Forest, creating a series of works that celebrated the enduring relationship between trees, woods and people, and explored imaginative ways to keep our arboreal neighbours in our daily lives (*see* Christine Mackey on page 91, Assemble on pages 128—129, Kurt Jackson on pages 84—85 and Owen Griffiths on page 159).

Between 2017 and 2018, the Kent Downs Area of Outstanding Natural Beauty (AONB) commissioned The Ash Project as an 'urgent cultural response to the devastating effects of ash dieback', including artistic commissions, community engagement, an

David Nash stands among the *Ash Dome* which he planted in 1977 and continued to shape and record. One of Britain's most important sculptors and land artists, he realised early in his career that wood was right for him: 'I wanted a material which would inform the work or be a partner in it. When I was first working I was just dominating the material – I'd cut it to shape, I'd paint it, sand it … then I thought: why don't you just look at the wood, where it's coming from? Working with wood is so special because it is something that has grown, a life force that weaves earth and light into the tree's body.' Photograph by Rob Fraser.

ASH DOME

Maentwrog, North Wales

Ash to Ash was made in 2018 by the artists Ackroyd & Harvey and is a celebration of the ash tree, the most common tree in the Kent Downs, and a memorial in response to ash dieback. The sculpture was commissioned by The Ash Project and sited in White Horse Wood Country Park, in the Kent Downs Area of Outstanding Natural Beauty. Photo courtesy of Kent Downs AONB.

PAUL NASH 1889-1946
One of the most important landscape artists of the 20th century, Nash was also a leading figure in the development of Modernism in British art. As an official war artist in the First World War, his paintings of shattered trees mocked the ambitions of war. His later work explored Surrealism, notably *Event on the Downs*, which showed a giant tennis ball next to a twisted tree stump.

online archive and a plan for landscape restoration. Kent has been badly affected by ash dieback and aerial photos of the ash woodlands are truly shocking, with the defoliated ash reaching up like bleached coral amidst the other trees in leaf. The wider community, including schools, were involved in ash coppicing, block printing and green woodworking with ash, along with visits to local ash woods. They also created an Ash Archive of memories, images and artefacts that record 'the beauty of ash in the landscape and in our lives before it is too late'.

Making with wood

> We could not well have a wagon, a cart, a coach or a wheel-barrow, a plough, a harrow, a spade, an axe, or a hammer, if we had no Ash.
>
> *William Cobbett, The Woodlands* (1825)

Wood has furnished our world for millennia. Our long history of making things out of trees is undergoing a revival, as people seek out natural materials, ways of life and processes in an age of ubiquitous plastic and mass production. Tree fairs and festivals are widespread, offering live chainsaw sculpture, tree climbing, archery, wines made of berries or sap, forest mushrooms and nuts, local charcoal, forest eggs and meat, wooden spoons, bowls, jewellery and ornaments.

People love working with wood. They enjoy the varying smells, texture and different qualities of tree species: they can be strong and solid but also pliable and malleable. Wood can be sculpted, shaved, cut, sanded or gouged. Woodland crafts such as hurdle-making and green woodworking have been quietly practised for centuries, but are now enjoying a renewed popularity. There is also a younger generation of designer-makers working with wood, exploring traditional and contemporary technology, sourcing wood as locally as they can, and relishing the natural forms and characteristics of different trees, accepting wood as it is but also manipulating it into extraordinary forms. Wood that is often overlooked for its 'imperfections' is becoming widely used, as designer-makers like Alice Blogg, Sebastian Cox and John Eadon celebrate the holes and burrs and cracks that tell the story of growth, decay and renewal.

Highly skilled craftspeople are not only finding their products

Laura Ellen Bacon's sculpture at RSPB South Essex Marshes. Having access to woods from a young age is what turned Laura into an artist: 'The scent of the wood floor and the tangling nature of twigs revealed a creative sense that is still potent for me today. I spent my youngest years nestling into woody nooks and branchy havens, wherever I could find them, making spaces of my own.' Photograph courtesy of Laura Ellen Bacon and RSPB South Essex Marshes.

Milling: the varied works of Sebastian Cox combine tradition and conservation with contemporary design. All the objects he makes express the textures and patterns of wood. The maker's job, he believes, is to retain these natural characteristics, including so-called 'imperfections'. Photograph courtesy of Sebastian Cox.

more in demand, but also their skills, as people want to learn from them. What was once the grinding necessity of rural life – making simple things from readily available materials to serve an immediate need – has become, for some, a new lease of life. Making your own chair, carving a spoon, weaving a willow basket – all these crafts can be learned, if not mastered, by spending time in our woods with the experts.

We still mostly live in an age when the things we buy are removed from the people and processes that made them. We can challenge the status quo – quite literally – by taking matters into our own hands and making things. It satisfies our creativity and our desire for authenticity and provenance. In a digital world, creating with wood is distinctly analogue, even an act of resistance. And spending time out in the woods allows the possibility of deeper immersion in nature, whiling away the long summer evenings, hearing the owls at night, feeling the morning dew, dancing to drums or just sitting quietly on a log in the sun.

Celebrating our trees

We celebrate trees with art and in words, both as a symbol of nature and as individual living beings, creating rituals that express our relationship to a particular place or tree – we gather round trees, in groves, walk in the shelter of woods. Pleasingly, there is a growing number of tree events and activities around the UK, including Apple Day, Tree Dressing Day, National

Timber stacks (*left*) at Whitney Sawmills, Herefordshire. Established in the 1990s by local craftsman Will Bullough, the sawmill has grown to become a respected supplier of timber. As well as supporting rural employment and skills, it supplies timber to a variety of projects, including the restoration of *HMS Victory*. With the charity Woodland Heritage, the aim is to increase the supplies of timber from well-managed UK and European woodlands, and to help promote the sustainability of native timber. Photograph courtesy of Whitney Sawmills.

Alice Blogg is a designer-maker who uses locally sourced or native timbers as much as possible in her workshop in West Dorset. 'The ash for the stools comes from the woodland a minute's walk from my workshop. The guy who planted the tree 35 years ago was the same guy who cut the tree down. It went from a felled tree to turned stools in two weeks.' The bench she made from oak (*below*), explores the natural tannin content of the oak to create a gradient of colours. Photography courtesy of Alice Blogg.

For the communities around Chelsea Road in Sheffield the act of decorating and celebrating this elm tree was also an act of resistance: by expressing their affection for the tree they were also helping to protect it from chainsaws and misguided decisions. Photograph by Fran Halsall.

A SIGN OF PEACE 1947
The huge Christmas tree installed annually in Trafalgar Square is donated to the people of Britain by the city of Oslo in Norway. This has happened every year since 1947 as a token of gratitude for British support to Norway during the Second World War. The tree remains in place until just before the Twelfth Night when it is taken down for recycling. The tree is chipped and composted, to make mulch.

Tree Week and wassailing our orchards, which all provide a date in our busy calendar for us to be able to stop, appreciate and celebrate the life-sustaining gifts of trees and woods. There is even a Timber Festival, started in 2018, a weekend of discussions, activities and music set in the National Forest to explore 'what forests and woodlands can mean to us and how we can re-imagine our relationship with our environment'.

Ancient trees are often celebrated for their spiritual significance. The tree of life, or world tree, is a symbol of immortality and fertility across all faiths and the focus of many religious festivals. Buddha sat under the Bodhi (a fig) tree when

OUR TREE DRESSING WORLD

The simplicity of tying strips of cloth or yarn to a tree is universal. The act of dressing a tree binds us to it and celebrates the unique role that trees have in our neighbourhoods. The old Celtic custom of the 'clootie tree' (*above middle*) echoes the practice in Japan of decorating trees (*above right*) with strips of white paper, called *tanzaku*, with wishes and poems written on them, or in Islington Green in London (*above left*) where the artist Svar Simpson was commissioned to represent the cultural importance of trees in the community. The Buddhist tradition of tying colourful ribbons around the trunk of the Bodhi tree (*top right*) is as wonderful as the modern fashion of 'yarn bombing' at Killerton in Devon (*top left*), covering an apple tree in 400 knitted leaves and woolly wildlife to celebrate Apple Day. The first weekend in December is now the time for community groups and schools to gather for their annual Tree Dressing. Common Ground launched the festival in 1990, by decorating a plane tree in central London, on the corner of Shaftesbury Avenue and High Holborn. In the wake of the devastating storm of October 1987, in which some 15 million trees crashed to the ground, the idea was to bring people together from all cultures to celebrate city and country trees and the natural world.

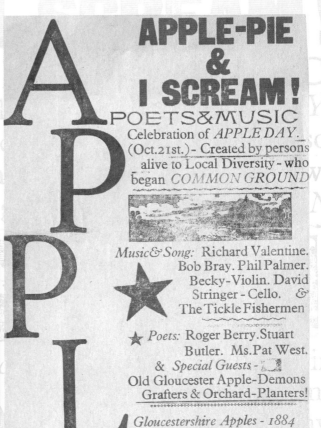

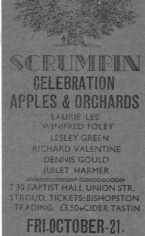

STROUD APPLE DAY POSTERS
by Dennis Gould, 1995–2018

Dennis Gould is a poet, peace activist and printer from Stroud, Gloucestershire. His distinctive letterpress style is a continuation of his cut-and-paste work from the late 1970s, when he set up his Woodblock Letterpress workshop. Printing is Dennis's way of getting ideas into the world, and in response to Apple Day he has for many years sent Common Ground the wonderful posters he printed for local events in Stroud.

Wassailing the apple trees at Strongs Orchard, Dorset. 'Wassail' is from Anglo-Saxon and means 'to be healthy' and wassailing is an old celebration to encourage a good crop. It usually takes place after dark on Old Twelfth Night, 17 January. Photograph by Graham Shackleton.

he gained enlightenment. Tu BiShvat is the New Year of the Trees in the Jewish tradition, when trees are planted and celebrated, and the Sidra Tree is an important symbol in the Arab world. These deep and diverse cultural associations provide a rich basis for tree festivities across the globe.

In Japan, the arrival of the cherry blossom in the spring – *sakura zensen* – is monitored, mapped and eagerly anticipated for weeks. People also celebrate *Tanabata*, known as the Star Festival, by writing wishes and poetry on *tanzaku* (small pieces of paper) and hanging them from trees.

The decoration of trees on festive days, such as Christmas and May Day (when the maypole is used to symbolise a tree), are old traditions in many parts of the world. The Arbor Tree, a black poplar in the centre of the village of Aston-on-Clun in Shropshire, was permanently adorned with flags which were renewed in May each year in a ceremony whose origins have largely been forgotten. In Appleton in Cheshire, late June sees the 'bawming of the thorn', an old custom involving the decoration of a hawthorn tree by local children with ribbons and garlands. Other tree-dressing rituals, such as the shoe tree in Armstrong Park in Newcastle or near Studley Green in the Chilterns, are not so ancient and perhaps less aesthetically pleasing!

Tree dressing is a powerful way of expressing our relationship

The apple is a symbol of what is being lost in many aspects of our lives: Apple Day shows that anyone can take positive action towards change. Each year on Apple Day, alongside tasting, juicing, baking, pruning and grafting, an imaginative array of games and cultural activities take place. Let's make Apple Day an official bank holiday in the UK!

Celebrating the transformative power of trees, Whispering Woods is a performance group of aerialists, musicians and storytellers that create one-off shows out in the landscape, often with trees and woods as an integral part of the imaginative and emotional journey. Photograph courtesty of Whispering Woods.

with trees. Tree Dressing Day (on the first weekend in December) has grown to become much more than an expression of a love for trees. It is a chance for the whole community to gather and celebrate the leafy friends we all have in common. It's also a chance for communities to reflect on the social and cultural history of their local area, and the role trees have played in shaping this story.

Play: wild time in the woods

In the space of a single generation, children's play has moved indoors. The American author Richard Louv has coined the term 'nature deficit disorder' to explain this shift, suggesting that over-protective care, loss of local open space and increased time spent indoors staring at screens have deprived many of

The shoe tree in Newcastle is an old sycamore in Armstrong Park. There are lots of stories about how and why the shoes started appearing, but it is thought that over twenty years ago some young people celebrated the end of their exams by throwing their shoes into the branches. Whether they landed there accidentally or not, we might never know, but since then Newcastle's school leavers have carried on the practice. Sometimes, a shoe harvest is carried out to maintain the health of the tree!

contact with the natural world. As a result, we are likely to have shorter attention spans, have less microbial variety in our immune systems, be more prone to suffer from depression, obesity and stress, and generally lack respect for nature.

Fear is a major factor: stranger danger, traffic, all those unknown risks. Roaming distance has shrunk by 90 per cent in a generation. There are real dangers both in the wild and closer to home, so we need to address these as a community. Lack of time is another major problem – lack of parents' time, lack of school time; we are always busy with something else. Green space is also vanishing from towns, including the edgelands, leaving fewer places to play outside. Now experiences are bought, downloaded, updated, forever faster with the promise of better. The anodyne entertainment of twentieth-century television has now exploded into the parallel universe of small tech screen time, sucking us all in with its irresistible gravity.

The answer is to confront these barriers and offer children enticing adventures in the natural world. The Wild Network does this with inspirational outdoor activities and resources, encouraging its followers to 'rewild childhood' and grow 'Wild Time' by redesigning our lives and communities to allow more space for nature. The Forestry Commission has also seized the opportunity for natural play. Where once their forest managers would have cleared away fallen trees, rope swings and dens, now they actively encourage them, with due concern for safety. Their

POOH STICKS 1928
Pooh sticks was invented by AA Milne in The House at Pooh Corner. The World Pooh Sticks Championships are now played annually on the River Thames at Day's Lock in Oxfordshire.

The simple joy of climbing trees – there is no better way to get to grips with trees than to clamber all over them, feel their bark, explore their architecture, spend time up off the ground in the canopy.

'Nature Play' website offers practical ideas for informal play in woods, from the obvious tree-climbing and log-balancing to secret paths, willow domes and creating homes for imaginary forest dwellers. The Woodland Trust also embraces the world of outdoor play with their 'Nature Detectives' initiative, while the National Trust encourages outdoor play in its '50 things to do before you're 11 ¾'.

The Forest School movement is perhaps the most cohesive and long-standing project to move thousands of children and young people outside, arguing that the natural environment is a stimulating classroom for all kinds of learning. The movement has grown in the UK from the early 2000s, drawing on a long history of British and European outdoor learning. Forest School is a long-term process which develops a relationship between the pupils and the natural world, fostering 'resilient, confident, independent and creative learners'. Run by trained and qualified staff, it crucially allows pupils to take 'supported risks' and so gain access to the wilder corners of the natural world. Rather than having a set curriculum, it takes a learner-centred approach and follows the changing moods and seasons of nature. This approach

Text within the image:

AND MY OLD FEET ARE ROOTED TO THIS PLACE

MY PEN CAN

AT THE Y VALLEY EVERYBODY STOPPED TO ASK WHY

THEY FOUND A GOLDEN ONE

THIS TREE IS BIGGER THAN EARTH

ONCE UPON A TIME WHEN THE LAKE WASN'T DRY FISH FILLED IT REEDS GREW IN IT SWANS SWAM IN IT HERRINGS FISHED IN IT AND THOSE MEMORIES TODAY. KEEP THE LAKE GOING, DAY BY DAY BY DAY

MY PEN CAN TAKE ME TO ANOTHER PLACE

I AM LOST IN MIST WITHOUT THE PATH

AND MY OLD HEART IS A WOODEN CHEST

A FANTASTICAL MAP OF SPINNEY WILD WOODS

CAMBRIDGE CURIOSITY AND IMAGINATION

ELENA AREVALO MELVILLE

A WILD EXCHANGE

certainly addresses 'nature deficit disorder' and brings human history full circle – here we are back in the woods, surrounded by wildlife, learning to live in nature again. In some state schools, such as the Dorset Studio School, the principles of Forest School have been absorbed into the daily curriculum.

Lifelong learning

As the author Robert Pogue Harrison points out, forests are outside the ambit of civilisation: places of enigma and paradox; places of profanity but also sacred; places of lawlessness but also natural justice; places of danger and abandonment but also enchantment and recovery. So a wood is a fine place to embark on a journey of discovery.

This is no surprise, especially when we consider the great

In the summer of 2015, The Spinney Primary School, in Cherry Hinton, Cambridge, invited the poet Jackie Kay and the artist Elena Arevalo Melville to explore the Spinney Wild Woods. Together with the students at the school, they created *A Poem of a Dream of the Woods* and made this *Fantastical Map of Spinney Wild Woods*. The project was run by Cambridge Curiosity and Imagination and the artist Deb Wilenski.

The outdoor music pavilion and learning space at St John's primary school in Lacey Green, was designed by Clementine Blakemore and made at Grymsdyke Farm in Buckinghamshire, a research facility, fabrication workshop and living-working space for architects, artists and designers.

transformative power of woods and trees. We even borrow words from trees and wood to express ourselves: how we feel rooted in places or sometimes need to turn over a new leaf, or how we learn from trees of knowledge and belong to family trees. Something enchanting happens when we step into the dappled shade of a wood; we feel an intimate kind of magic under the canopy of leaves and branches. And when we climb trees our perspective changes, literally and metaphorically: a different view brings with it a different mood, a different feeling.

But this knowledge isn't new. Our ancestors knew it. That's why so many place names and folk stories are inspired by woods and trees. William Shakespeare wrote trees and woods into *Macbeth* and *As You Like It*. It is also why he chose a woody setting for *A Midsummer Night's Dream*, a play populated by fairies and magic and moods which shapeshift along with the identities of the characters.

This transformative power fires our imaginations and inspires wonder today. When a character in a story enters a wood, they will seldom emerge unchanged. Some acquire wisdom, some gain power, others are lost or found. Our woods offer an alternative arena in which we can play out our human dramas.

FOREST SCHOLL

After attending a Forest School Leaders course at Bridgwater College, Somerset, in 2014, Stuart and Desiree Young started searching for a wood where they could start their own Forest School. Although it was a frustrating start, they found Hakeford Woods, fell in love with it, and started discussing a lease arrangement with the charity that owned it, Wildlife Woodlands. They also had to get planning permission for a change of use to include educational work.

Hakeford Forest School is now a Community Interest Company (CIC), which means it is a limited company that benefits the community rather than private shareholders. They work with adults of all ages and young people with emotional and behavioural difficulties who have been excluded from mainstream schools.

There is a growing need for access to outdoor education and therapeutic opportunities for people of various ages. Shortages in funding, transport difficulties and issues around the requirements of the curriculum and assessment mean schools can be reluctant to let children out as much as they have done in the past.

Most beneficial for the long-term wellbeing and self-esteem of students, as well as their resilience, is what the Youngs describe as 'full fat' forest school: these are full days in the woods on a long-term basis, when young people are able to develop experiences and knowledge of the woods, which are places of space and freedom. There are no walls and they can get away from one another when necessary, finding their own space.

Over time, the students also help carry out simple woodland-management jobs: coppicing or building paths and gathering places.

Because funding for young people is volatile, Desiree and Stuart Young are adding new types of activities and programmes at Hakeford Woods: parent and toddler groups, home-schooling and woodcraft. Through connections with local charities like the Wildlife Trust they are also increasing the number of volunteers getting involved. They also want to run sessions for adults with mental health difficulties, referred through housing and homeless organisations, NHS and probation services.

HAKEFORD FOREST SCHOOL: hakefordwoods.co.uk
THE FOREST SCHOOL ASSOCIATION: forestschoolassociation.org

Common Ground's Seasonal Schools project collaborates with teachers in order to find imaginative ways to reconnect the curriculum with daily experiences of the seasons, nature and places that are near or inside the school grounds. Photograph by Graham Shackleton.

Perhaps we feel more free in the woods, no longer constrained by our daily routines and habits, at once both more expansive and more intimate than in our daily lives or in a village hall.

Woods are also increasingly seen as a 'facilitating environment' for personal and social-development activities. Perhaps all these new ideas and activities are nurturing a new kind of wood culture that suits the needs and pressures of twenty-first century life.

We need to re-accustom ourselves to nature, to feel at home in the woods and widen our circle of experience to include wild places and processes. Of course, traditional conservation volunteer groups offer people meaningful work and engagement with their local woods, to the benefit of the wildlife, the volunteers and other people who use the wood. Friends Groups are a particularly popular and effective way of getting involved with your local wood. Practical activities such as work on paths, coppicing and clearing brambles are a good way to get people together, as are events such as bluebell picnics, birdsong walks and exploring the wood's natural history and archaeology.

Friends of particular trees or woods can also become their Guardians when, for whatever reason, they are threatened. For

'I went through some quite severe depressions over the years, and if it wasn't for the trees I don't know if I'd be here. It's as simple as that.' So says Neill Mapes, a woodsmith who has been teaching people about wood and woodland management for many years. 'Passing things on, working with trees and in woodland, and working with the timber I think is very fundamental to people. That's why it's so important that we have public spaces that we can all gravitate to – even if it's just to go away for half an hour and sit among the trees and just switch off.' Photograph courtesy of the Woodland Trust and Neill Mapes.

example, when Chopwell Wood in Gateshead was earmarked for sale by the Forestry Commission in 2011, the residents tied yellow ribbons to doors, gates and hedges to create a ring of protection around the wood. Ribbons lined the route into the Wood and were worn by protesters, horses and even dogs. About 1,500 people protested and the Friends sent a representative to meet the Independent Forestry Panel in Hexham to put the case for continued public ownership and enjoyment.

At Fingle Woods in Devon (*see* pages 144–45), the Woodland Trust's site manager sees the wood as embedded in the local community: 'We have been keen from the start of the Fingle project to share our knowledge and understanding of the woods as work and surveys progress. This has been a two-way process with the local community, ranging from hosting monthly meetings in the local pub or walks in the wood to discuss current management, the most recent biodiversity discovery or the amazing history from excavations to interpreting academic tomes, the changing climate and its growing impact on the landscape – indeed, all the elements that comprise such a complex project. There is no doubt that both staff and community alike have worked together to create a rich sense of ownership.'

There is one hurdle, however. How often do we hear a great idea for a woodland activity, only to hear in the next breath

Making a sound sculpture with the Neroche Woodlanders near Taunton in Somerset. The Neroche Woodlanders describe their approach as 'connecting people with themselves and others through simply being in nature'. Amongst the many activities on offer, there is 'Wild Learning', which is a sort of Forest School for adults, based on the four pillars of the John Muir Award: 'explore, discover, conserve, share'. Photographs courtesy of Neroche Woodlanders.

that it is unfeasible 'because of health and safety'? Games and outings once common and unregulated have fallen foul of an excessive aversion to risk. We seem to have lost our ability to make judgements about danger – to assess risk. No tree can be guaranteed as safe. Yet if we are to develop a culture closer to nature, we need to be able to assess risk better in our daily lives.

Natural Health Service

Nature is good for us! We've known that for a while. It's a bit like saying we need oxygen or water to live. Until the late twentieth century, outdoor spaces around most hospitals were considered part of the healing environment and patients could walk in gardens, orchards, even hospital farms. But more recently, the priority has been to create a sterile medical environment indoors, and the benefits of a natural environment have been ignored.

There is now an evidence-based movement to take healing

Blarbuie Woods, in the grounds of Argyll and Bute Hospital, was restored by Reforesting Scotland, the NHS, Argyll Green Woodworkers Association, the Scottish Association for Mental Health and Lochgilphead Community Council. It was opened as a public park in 2007, with all-abilities paths, regular 'health walks' and other events now taking place. Photographs courtesy of Blarbuie Woodland Enterprise.

outdoors and once again encourage contact with the natural world. Unlike 'hard' urban environments, nature engages our attention without demanding anything of us, so we are able to awaken the senses whilst also reducing stress and allowing our own healing processes to develop. Woods and parks, meadows and beaches – all natural places can contribute to our alternative NHS: the Natural Health Service, to complement our medical provision. According to the Office for National Statistics, UK woods already save us nearly a billion pounds a year in health costs just from pollution removal alone.

Many outdoor spaces can have therapeutic effects, but trees and woods have a particular role to play: they are protective and sheltering, with room enough for many; they offer a haven for the solitary wanderer and a place to meet friends; they are a rich source of sights, sounds, smells and textures, a place of dappled sun and shade; they are often quiet enough to hear birdsong, the rustle of leaves or the snap of a twig; an ancient old tree or an expansive forest can inspire awe and take us out of our immediate circumstances into a deeper sense of time and space.

The benefits of trees, woods and all green spaces are especially helpful right at the point of treatment, in our hospitals and clinics. The wider setting of a hospital – its grounds, views, paths and landscape – all contribute to a sense of connection with nature. Even confined spaces between buildings and in courtyards can

Based in Edinburgh, SEASONS is a city council service offering a variety of activities for adults who wish to have support with their mental health and emotional wellbeing. The service offers a range of creative and social activities, trips and time in green space, including conservation and tree-planting. SEASONS service has been supported with nature-connection activities by Edinburgh's community park ranger service, the National Trust for Scotland and Jupiter Artland Education Foundation.

be designed to offer views of trees and shrubs and places to sit, outside the busy clinical hospital environment. When designing therapeutic spaces, we should remember the healing power of nature – make use of trees and flowers, create places that feel special, embrace the dynamic rhythms of nature

Even within our medical facilities, a tree can transform a place. A single magnolia can change a dull courtyard into a glorious eruption of flowers (Salisbury Hospital); or a single pine can reach up several stories and offer new views on every level (Ninewells Hospital, Dundee). It is the particular mission of Maggie's Centres nationwide to provide 'the architecture of hope'. Offering free practical and emotional support for people affected by cancer, they are places where trees have a central role in the architectural spaces, planted and growing to lift the spirits and set the scene for people to draw on inner strengths.

Natural surroundings have been found to be particularly helpful for alleviating depression, owing to factors as basic as exposure to daylight and walking. Woods can also offer opportunities for so many more proactive approaches, from mindfulness practice to participation in woodland work. The Japanese idea of *shinrin-yoku* (or 'forest bathing') has been practised in Japan since the 1980s, and has become such an important part of preventive health care and healing, that the government has incorporated it into annual health programming and spending.

NEW WOODLAND COMMUNITIES

A group takes part in a week-long accredited strawbale building course at Hill Holt Wood, as part of the Our Bright Future project funded by the National Lottery Community Fund and led by The Wildlife Trusts.

Hill Holt Wood near Lincoln is a social enterprise and registered charity that owns and manages 65 acres of ancient woodland and 10 acres of wet grassland, with a further 1,000 acres that it manages for a variety of landowners, including the Woodland Trust and local authorities.

Hill Holt is underpinned by the ethos of helping people and caring for the environment. Education of young people makes up half of the activities at Hill Holt Wood, including a study programme for 16–19-year-olds that is Ofsted inspected. Most students have an education health and care plan, with several students under 16 attending up to two days a week for alternative education. Hill Holt also runs a woodland mental health and ecotherapy project, with 100 places a month.

Alongside education and therapy, Hill Holt Wood provides countryside management services to a local authority, including litter-picking and gardening. It also has an event space with catering facilities that is well used by local schools and other organisations. There are plans to open a preschool and a space for residential artists.

HILL HOLT: hillholtwood.co.uk
OUR BRIGHT FUTURE: ourbrightfuture.co.uk

At the Maggie's Centre in Oldham, a silver birch has become the centre of attention, casting shadows and offering ever-changing shifts of light and pattern. The building itself is also the first permanent building constructed from hardwood cross-laminated timber, designed by dRMM Architects.

Woods can offer a completely different path to healing, a chance to step out of the cares of normal life, a campfire in a clearing. They are more permeable places: people can come and go as they please. This is something they have discovered at Foundry Wood, a community woodland in Warwickshire, which organises weekly ecotherapy sessions and other activities that incorporate the 'Five Ways to Wellbeing' recommended by the New Economics Foundation: *Connect*, *Be Active*, *Take Notice*, *Keep Learning*, *Give*. Visitors to Foundry Wood often say they've 'found their tribe or family' because of the shared sense of purpose they find working outside with other people – an experience that might be lacking in daily life. Kath Pasteur, who helped establish Foundry Wood, says: 'We've taken a neglected space and we've transformed it into a thriving community woodland. And we're doing the same with people. We're taking neglected and isolated people and we're bringing them into this space and creating a community that can enjoy this woodland.'

The healing power of nature has even been recognised at the level of microbiology in the Human Urban Microbiome Initiative (HUMI), which seeks to 'understand and re-create the immune-boosting power of high-quality, biodiverse green spaces in our cities to maximise population health benefits, bring significant savings to health budgets, while delivering gains for biodiversity.' Our bodies are host to billions of microorganisms that keep us healthy; likewise the natural world around us is pervaded and serviced by co-operative microorganisms. These healthy ecologies can be compromised and depleted in urban areas, so the initiative aims for healthy microbiomes in our surroundings that support healthy microbiomes within our own bodies. If we are to live our lives in better local environments that reconnect more people to nature, understanding that we all occupy the same ecological continuum is an excellent place to start.

Towards a wood culture

We actively seek out woods for particular purposes such as walking, playing and learning. Spending time amongst the trees adds a special quality to these activities. The woods are not just neutral spaces; rather they are positively supportive and nurturing, both stimulating and relaxing, holding yet liberating. Woods bring out the wild in us. They provide an immersive experience quite different to our normal surroundings of houses, cars and supermarkets. They offer a complex structure, sometimes like a cathedral, sometimes more like a maze, with gently shimmering details of light and shade, leaf and sky, trunks dividing into branches and ever finer fractal twigs and flowers, with birds and insects weaving to and fro. Trees and woods are also a very versatile base material for our creative imagination: we project our emotions and dreams onto them, or from them we shape our ideas and visions.

People value woods for all sorts of intangible qualities and plenty of more tangible ones, such as riding bikes, walking, having picnics, building dens, escaping from the pressures of twenty-first-century living. Because woods are so popular and beneficial to us, the Woodland Trust developed a 'Woodland Access Standard' to measure how many people had access to woods. There are two criteria: access to a wood of at least 2 hectares within 500 m of where you live and access to a wood of at least 20 hectares within 4 km. Only 21 per cent of us live close to a small accessible wood, whilst 73 per cent of us live a

'Spud Wood' in Lymm, Cheshire, is on the site of a former potato field. When this 'millennium wood' was due for thinning, the owners (the Woodland Trust) gave a Community Interest Company, the Friends of Spud Wood, a licence to 'cut and collect'. To join this 'wood allotment' scheme, members pay an annual fee that covers the basic costs of administration, and in return they have a sustainable fuel source on their doorstep and are helping improve the biodiversity of the wood.

short walk or drive from a bigger wood. The Trust's conclusion is that 'too few people have high-quality accessible woodland near to where they live'.

The problem appears to be threefold: we do not have enough woods; many private woods are not open to the public; most people live in cities far from woods. Access would be better if all private woods were open to the public (as is the case under the Scottish Outdoor Access Code), which would allow 55 per cent of the population to access small woods and 88 per cent to access larger woods. In 2017, a new Charter for 'Trees, Woods and People' recommended: 'Landowners should receive support and encouragement to overcome legal and practical barriers to allow public access to their woods'. The Tree Charter and the Woodland Trust's conclusions about access can be used in local planning to indicate where to target incentives to improve access to woods and to create new community woods.

Historically, the traditional forms of ownership in Britain were the Crown, aristocracy or wealthy individuals. Common people exercised rights to certain woodland produce from other people's woods, but this largely ended with the enclosure of common land. In the twentieth century, the government stepped in to create state-owned forests (the Forestry Commission) and became the largest landowner in the country. Charity ownership has also grown in recent decades, particularly through the

THOMAS HARDY
1840–1928
With its title borrowed from Shakespeare's 'As You Like It', Thomas Hardy published 'Under the Greenwood Tree' in 1872. It was the first of his 'Wessex Novels', which also included The Woodlanders published in 1887.

LEEDS COPPICE WORKERS

Leeds Coppice Workers (LCW) is a co-operative that provides locally sourced firewood and charcoal. There are eight members (and five regular workers) who bring a wealth of different skills and experience. This enables the group to carry out a number of varied tasks through the calendar year: coppice restoration, hedge-laying, contract-felling, tree-planting, Forest School for all ages, craft workshops and consultancy. It aims to engage local people with community woods and demonstrate how they can be managed in a sustainable and ecologically sound way. They look after woodlands on behalf of Yorkshire Wildlife Trust and Leeds City Council in three primary locations: Hetchell Wood (near Thorner), Townclose Hills (in Kippax) and Castle Hill (near Micklefield). Alongside, they manage woodlands in Sicklinghall, East Keswick, Water Haigh, Seckar and Bramhope. LCW believes passionately in the positive impact that outdoor work can have on wellbeing, and run monthly volunteer days to facilitate an inspiring and positive space for both learning and therapeutic outdoor activity.

LEEDS COPPICE WORKERS: leedscoppiceworkers.co.uk

A community group on a guided tour at Hooke Park in Dorset. The woodland is owned and managed by the Architectural Association, but accessible via a number of bridleways and open to the public during various events that take place throughout the year. Photograph by Graham Shackleton.

National Trust and the Woodland Trust, but this represents less than 5 per cent of our woods.

Ownership matters because the owner of a wood ultimately decides what happens there. About a quarter of the woodland in the UK is owned by the state and managed by non-ministerial government departments: Forestry England, Forestry and Land Scotland, Natural Resources Wales, and the Forest Service of Northern Ireland. All the state-owned woods are covered by management plans and are certified under the UK Woodland Assurance Scheme (UKWAS), so they should be in good condition and under active management. Most of these woods are also open to the public.

Private woodland makes up nearly three-quarters of woodland in the UK. In England, a further 6 per cent of woodland is owned by local authorities, and almost half of these local authorities have no strategy or plan for the woods in their care. Lack of funding and staff are always key challenges – woods are not seen as an asset requiring proactive management, but rather as a liability only requiring reactive management for health and safety.

Local authorities are missing a trick: they could involve their constituents more fully by devolving management of their woods to local groups who want to establish social enterprises

Storey G2, an arts organisation in Lancaster, commissioned the artist Layla Curtis to create a mobile app, called 'Trespass', to tell the story of Freeman's Wood from the perspective of people who used it. Layla talked to local people about their personal memories of the site and how they regarded the area as common land. They also described how they felt when the landowner erected a metal fence around Freeman's Wood, and of how this, and the accompanying 'Keep Out, No Trespassing' signs affected the way the space is now used and accessed.

or community woodlands. But council officers often feel that the biggest barrier is the time it takes to build up organisations capable of effective management. Are these genuine cultural and economic barriers? Or is there a deeper, historic prejudice at play?

Contrary to popular belief, community ownership of the commons was not a free-for-all that naturally led to the 'tragedy of the commons'. Rather, they are specific areas with specific rights and responsibilities in which the participants regulate use. Actual ownership by the 'commoners' is not essential, but a commons system could exist on any land where the owner has agreed to the pooling of resources of labour and produce. For example, a local authority or individual landowner could open its woods up to local woodland workers for small-scale works.

Actual community ownership is very small in the UK, estimated at under 5,000 hectares (0.2 per cent of woodland). Compare this to France with 3 million hectares (20 per cent) owned by communes, or Germany with over 2 million hectares (19 per cent). We have a very different social and rural history to our Continental neighbours and it has left most of us with a much smaller stake in our land and much less of a wood culture today. From a low starting point in the 1990s, there has been a spectacular blossoming of community woodland groups in Britain. By 2013, there were over 650 such groups around the UK: over 300 in England, 200 in Scotland and over 150 in Wales. In Scotland there have been community buy-outs of forests and the establishment of the Community Woodlands Association (CWA) to support these enterprises. The CWA thinks community ownership is uniquely placed to deliver not only the usual benefits of forests but also 'a genuine opportunity for collective action, community empowerment and civic pride.' In Wales there has been funding for the Cydcoed programme to establish community woodland groups and ongoing support from Llais y Goedwig, 'the voice of community woodlands in Wales'. In England, although there isn't yet a community wood association, there is an increase in diverse initiatives across the country, supported by the Woodland Trust and the Making Local Woods Work partnership.

New kinds of projects are springing up all around the country, pioneering ways of working in the woods and renewing the role and meaning of trees in our cities and towns. All over the UK, in urban and rural places, there are firewood co-operatives, community-owned and -managed orchards, farms and woods, craftworkers' alliances, cutting-edge architectural and engineering experiments, health, wellbeing and education projects. It's happening because trees matter to people: they are meaningful and they are useful to our everyday lives.

This emergent wood culture is asking us to reimagine our relationship with trees and woods. We want our woods to be teeming with life and activity that seeks to sustain the natural world, bring us closer to nature and provide a living for a new generation of wood entrepreneurs. There are new forms of community ownership, too, and new opportunities for people to get out into their local woods to take part and help shape how and why they are managed.

Woodland Social Enterprises

Commercial forestry, like all industrialised agribusiness, has become large-scale and high-tech, often run by big corporations with big machinery. But as different wood cultures spread across the UK in the twenty-first century, more community groups are taking on ownership and responsibility for the management of woods. These Woodland Social Enterprises

OUR FOREST

The story of Kilfinan Community Forest Company (KCFC) began when villagers of Tighnabruaich, a village on the Cowal peninsula, in Argyll and Bute, started fundraising to buy the 125 hectares of Accrosan Plantation owned by Scotland's national forest estate. The idea was simple: to ensure that the land remained in public ownership so that the community could access the forest.

They were able to acquire the forest because of the National Forest Land Scheme initiated by Forestry Commission Scotland. The scheme was a response to the Land Reform (Scotland) Act 2003 which gives community organisations and non-governmental organisations (including housing bodies) the 'right to buy' or lease National Forest Land where they can increase public benefits.

Since KCFC took ownership, they have improved access by establishing paths and now have a regular Kilfinan Wayfarers Walkers group and other regular events, including a popular 'Dark Nights, Bright Lights' boat-burning ceremony! There is an ongoing programme of forestry education, with regular creative and practical workshops for people of all ages, particularly with young people from primary and secondary schools. There is an allotment scheme and a woodland crofting project in the forest, and KCFC have started to offer self-build sites for those who can demonstrate that they have the relevant skills to build their own affordable home in among the trees.

It is from all these different community activities that KCFC earns an income: leasing land for crofting and workshops space, the sale of self-build plots, the rental of a heated polytunnel. In 2015, KCFC purchased the Upper Acharossan Forest, so in addition to lease income they now own and manage 561 hectares of woodlands on behalf of the local community, from which they generate additional revenue from firewood, camping, commercial forestry, a sawmill for timber and hydro-electric generation.

KCFC have demonstrated that the resources of the forest are better used by the community at source, rather than diverted to distant, large-scale private owners. This improves the support that the forest can give to local employment, business and biodiversity, while also attracting new people to the area to walk and experience the forest for themselves.

KILFINAN COMMUNITY FOREST: kilfinancommunityforest.co.uk
FORESTRY AND LAND SCOTLAND: forestryandland.gov.scot
SCOTTISH FORESTRY: forestry.gov.scot

WOODFUEL CO-OP

Axewoods Co-operative started with a group of friends managing a woodland in east Devon, near the River Axe. No money changed hands: the group were paid in firewood, and the scheme was so successful that they ended up with more firewood than they needed themselves. That's why they decided to launch the 'log bank' scheme, which supplies free logs to families and individuals unable to afford to heat their homes.

The Axewoods Co-operative was formally established as an Industrial and Provident Society in 2010 and runs as a not-for-profit volunteer organisation helping its members secure their woodfuel needs, whilst addressing fuel poverty in the local area. There are now over 50 members, all of whom learn new skills and help coordinate volunteers, organise social activities and physically contribute to the management of woods. Long-term members have now developed both the technical skills, relevant qualifications and harvesting equipment to offer landowners a reliable service whilst providing local people with a rewarding new relationship with their local woods.

Since its formation in 2010, Axewoods has built a strong operational base and attracted an eclectic mix of members from a wide professional, age, gender and skills background.

The Axewoods members have worked with a variety of private and public landowners across east Devon: Clinton Devon Estates, East Devon District Council, the Forestry Commission, Donkey Sanctuary, National Trust, Offwell Woodland and Wildlife Trust. Overall, they manage about 100 hectares of broadleaved and conifer woodland producing approximately 60 tonnes of timber per year. This timber is either for members or local people in fuel poverty, provided for those referred to them by the local council, food banks, churches and other organisations.

Axewoods is a good example of how a simple 'logs for labour' operation can benefit the wider community and biodiversity of small woods. In times of austerity, the barriers of more 'formal' welfare systems are overcome to help people in need and widen access to woodlands, so that more people are able to experience the benefits of getting physical work in the woods.

AXEWOODS: axewoods.org.uk

An increasing number of woodland owners are inviting people from local communities to join in with management activities and workshops in the woods. The owners of this West Dorset wood host a 'woodlanders' group for light tasks in exchange for firewood, hazel poles and other coppice materials. All these initiatives are focused on making the wood more hospitable to wildlife in its hour of need. Photograph by Graham Shackleton.

(WSEs) are an inspiring source of ideas that demonstrate how working in the woods can deliver social, environmental and economic benefits directly to the woodland and the wider local community. Crucially, they reconnect people with local trees and woods, to the benefit of both.

We need a model of woodland enterprise that allows the best of both worlds: the knowledge of the professional forester plus the vast resource of volunteer engagement; the power and efficiency of high-tech machinery and the skill of the craftsman; using all angles to make the very best of a local resource.

What's particularly interesting about the variety of WSE projects across the country, is how they are defined by place and local people. These are not some top-down abstract idea. It is the search for local solutions to local problems in a particular landscape that shapes the purpose and character of each project. For example, in Scotland WSEs often have charitable status and operate in much larger forests (which they often own). But generally, across the UK, all WSEs tend to have a mission to remedy social issues, too – the things that the local or national government is not dealing with, ie poverty, isolation, physical and mental wellbeing. They often combine traditional methods of working timber and coppice along with using the

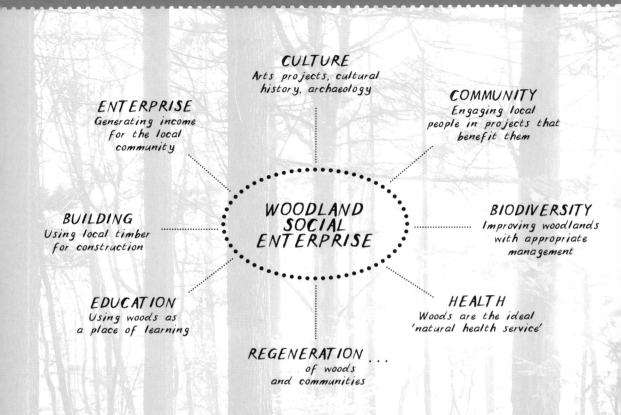

CULTURE
Arts projects, cultural
history, archaeology

COMMUNITY
Engaging local
people in projects that
benefit them

ENTERPRISE
Generating income
for the local
community

WOODLAND SOCIAL ENTERPRISE

BIODIVERSITY
Improving woodlands
with appropriate
management

BUILDING
Using local timber
for construction

EDUCATION
Using woods as
a place of learning

HEALTH
Woods are the ideal
'natural health service'

REGENERATION . . .
. . . of woods
and communities

wood as a setting for other activities, such as education, events or creative projects.

The distinguishing feature of any WSE, as opposed to a volunteer group, is that it also trades commercially. Those involved could be selling logs and timber, or services like education and health provision. They may be using their wood as a venue for events, courses, recreation, woodland burials and weddings, or offering their own experiences and expertise. Often all these activities are done in parallel, stacking up the benefits to generate multiple income streams. Funding for WSE can be derived from selling wood, grants, donations, loans, membership or community share issues.

WSEs also have much to offer the traditional forestry sector: they are bringing a new generation of entrepreneurs, ideas and skills to the woods, developing new markets for

woodland products and services, especially education, health and wellbeing. They are making woods more relevant to local people by offering new meanings, as well as upholding the obvious values of timber, fuel and craft working. Significantly, one-third of participants tend to be female entrepreneurs, in a traditionally male-dominated sector.

There are also several woodland educational organisations and social enterprises working on timber constructions, such as the Architectural Association at Hooke Park in Dorset, the Sylva Foundation in Oxfordshire, Grymsdyke Farm in Buckinghamshire, Elwy in Wales and the Wyre Forest Community Land Trust in Worcestershire, where craft, art and architecture are merging to create new approaches to building and enterprises that use local resources for local benefit.

'If you give people a reason to visit local woods, you can attract a new demographic of people.' So says Alex Tempest of The Woodland Presents, a not-for-profit social enterprise that runs a maker-space, courses, events and a community woodland group in Dartington, South Devon. Photograph courtesy of Alex Tempest.

LOG BOOK by Assemble, Chapter House, Lincoln, December 2017

For ten days in December, 2017, a group of skilled woodworkers worked in concert within the Lincoln Cathedral Chapter House to process wood from the round felled form into regular sections of timber. The work of the four hewers composed a process-led installation celebrating the technique and skill required to work with the material of the forest in its raw form. Set beneath the extraordinary timber structure hidden above the vaulted masonry ceiling that forms the Cathedral's Chapter House roof, the project exposed the vernacular architecture of the place, drawing out the beauty of the structure concealed within the building. *Log Book* was conceived and directed by Assemble and Common Ground, with lighting design by Katharine Williams, theatrical direction by Emily Lin, photography by Henrietta Williams and woodwork by Robert Ley, Anna Ley, James Irvine, Allan Eley, Shawn Farrell and Tom Wood.

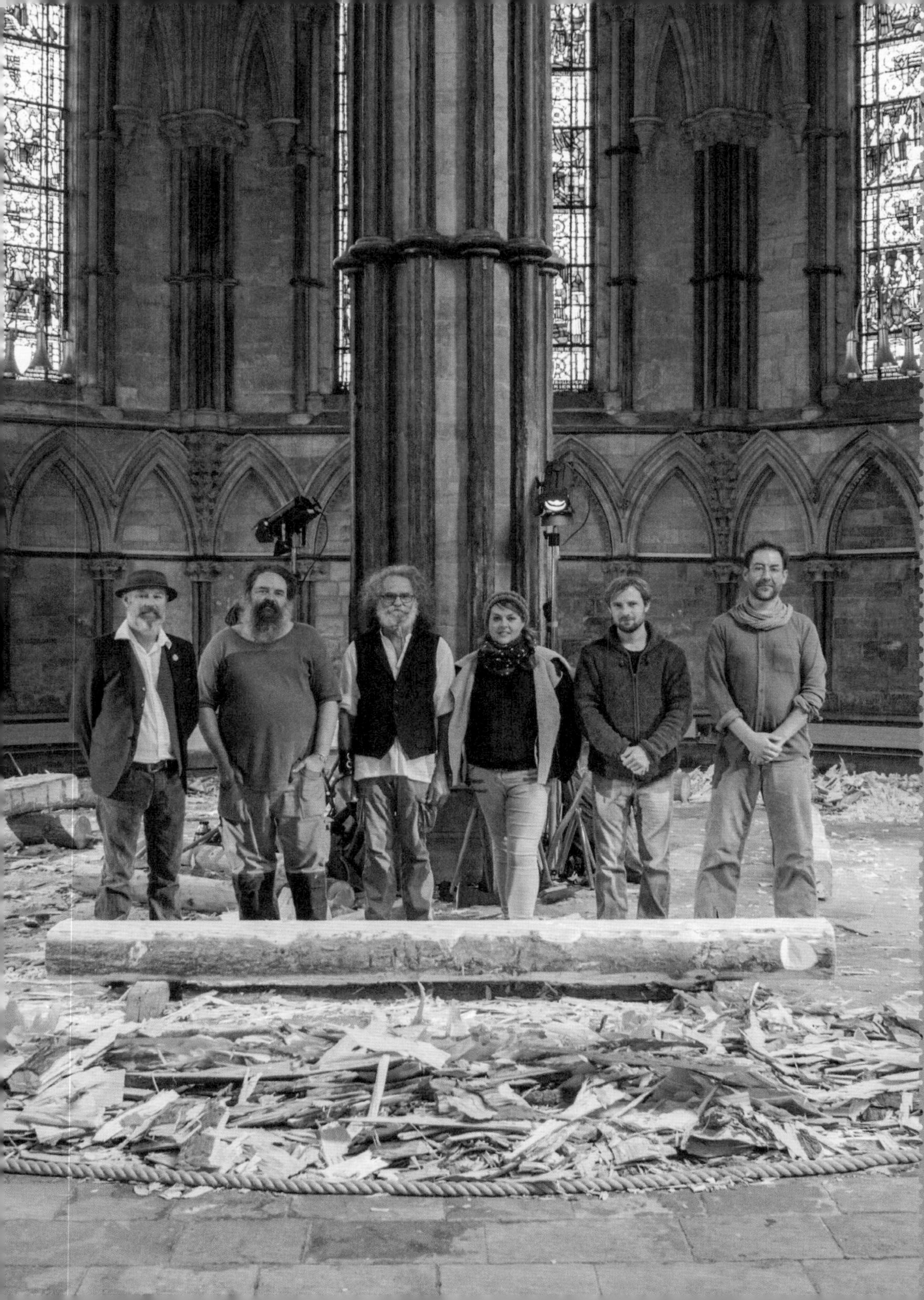

WORKING WITH TREES

THE ARTIST'S TREE by Alice Pattullo, 2016

In this artwork Alice Pattullo explores why trees are important to her work and life, providing the materials for her craft and feeding her imagination. It was originally designed for Common Ground and published in *LEAF!* newspaper.

Can we let forests flourish, but still take a cut? Although we can all appreciate wood sculpture, handmade furniture, books or timber-framed houses, we often wince at the sound of chainsaws or feel sickened at the sight of a clearfelled forest. People love forests but hate forestry!

If we are to develop a wood culture in Britain, we do need to embrace a wide range of arboreal experiences and woody contexts, celebrating and promoting trees of all sorts, from the tree at the end of the garden and the community orchard to the copse down the lane and the plantation on the far horizon. Trees will be very different in each situation, play different roles, fulfil different needs: we need them all. Woods and forests are dynamic places of change, never a static landscape, and this includes the growth, tending and felling of the working or 'productive forest'.

The F-word

Forestry is often overlooked and misunderstood. Foresters themselves have been content to get on, beavering away in the forest without telling the stories of their woods and their work. So why do we need to know more about trees and forestry now? Because our lives have to change. The human world we have built is not sustainable, it is crumbling, and the natural world is dying. We urgently need to renew our relationship with nature, to work with nature, and trees are a great place to start.

Britain had very little woodland in the nineteenth century and therefore a poor supply of home-grown timber, so we developed a reliance on global trade in timber supplies from the British Empire, Canada and Scandinavia. A supply network of rivers and canals, then railways and roads, allowed imported timber to reach all corners of

Clearfelling: an upland Sitka spruce plantation in Perthshire, Scotland.

the country and few places needed to rely on local woods. It was only during the First and then Second World Wars, when these timber imports were threatened, that we realised we needed to invest in planting, harvesting and processing our own timber to supply the war effort and national consumption.

The removal of our native hardwoods (oak, ash, beech) over centuries, followed by the sudden harvesting of all the best trees in wartime, creamed off the best-quality hardwood timber trees and left only a depleted gene pool for restoration. Today, we do not have the extensive forests, century-long vision and silvicultural traditions and services of other northern European countries. We need to rebuild our hardwood resources, both in quantity and quality, if we are to make full use of timber in the decades and centuries to come, and stop relying so heavily on imported hardwoods.

Although the home-grown softwood timber-milling industry has grown since the Second World War, supported by steady supplies from the Forestry Commission's maturing conifer forests, the quantity and quality must also be increased to develop our domestic softwood supply. In 2018, the UK produced about 11 million cubic metres of wood (93 per cent of it was softwood), imported about 49 million m^3 and exported 4 million m^3. This means we consumed 56 million m^3 of wood,

Thinning larch in a Plantation on an Ancient Woodland Site in Wiltshire. In the background, the harvester fells and cross-cuts the trees, then the forwarder picks up the cut logs and takes them to the timber stack.

importing about 81 per cent of it.

So what do we use it for? Of the 11 million tonnes felled, 56 per cent went into mills for sawn timber, 22 per cent went into woodfuel, 10 per cent went into panelboards (OSB, MDF) and the rest into other minor uses. Interestingly, only 4 per cent is used in paper production because most of the source material is recycled paper.

About one-fifth of our annual wood needs comes from UK forests. In fact, in 2017 we imported about £7.6 billion of 'forest products', which means the UK was second behind China as the world's largest net importer of wood.

The conifer plantations established from the 1960s to 1990s, which now form the majority of our productive woodland, are due to reach their peak in 2030, providing a potential harvest of around 18 million m³ per year. But because planting rates plummeted from 1988, these current softwood supplies will start to slowly decline. Furthermore, new planting in recent decades has focused more on native or deciduous trees, which are slow-growing hardwoods and will not fulfil our consumer appetite for wood.

In 2018 there were up to 16,000 people employed in forestry, with a further 27,000 in 'primary wood processing' (sawmills, panel-mills, etc). The forestry sector is worth around £2 billion,

Sessile oak in Ancient Semi-Natural Woodland in Gloucestershire, with a fine stand of oak and mixed understorey.

with one-third in forestry itself and two-thirds in the processing of wood. Compare this with agriculture: worth about £8 billion to the UK economy, employing almost 500,000 people, covering 72 per cent of the land and producing about half of our food; or the financial sector, which is worth £124 billion with over 1 million jobs.

It's been tough for the business of forestry in recent decades. From 1970 to 2010 the price for softwood fell in real terms by about two-thirds. Hardwood prices also fell by at least a third between 1989 and 2007.

But there are more promising signs: hardwood firewood and softwood chipwood (low-grade wood) have benefitted from the growth in woodfuel. And in 2018 timber sales also enjoyed a boom, with prices up a third.

Yet there are still many questions: how much can our present forests really contribute to a green economy of renewable resources? Since we only produce one-fifth of our own timber, how can this be sustainable? Should we use more wood in building affordable homes, or less? How much more forest do we need, and of what type?

We need more trees in more places – in gardens, parks, streets, hedges, fields, hillsides and uplands – and establishing a new generation of productive trees and forests is an important part of that vision. We have a century of experience planting and harvesting trees, with mistakes along the way, so perhaps we just need to learn the ecological and economic lessons and apply them to our new, more challenging situations. We need forestry that is fit for the future.

Preparing for climate disruption

The future is not what it used to be! We have enjoyed a relatively stable climate in the Holocene for about 12,000 years, enabling the development of extensive and complex ecosystems and civilisations. Climate is changing much more rapidly now than in previous millennia and trees growing from seeds today will mature many decades later in a significantly different climate. They will not be able to move to a more amenable climate and their offspring will not be able to migrate north fast enough to keep pace with projected climatic change.

The main impacts of climate change on our forests in the UK are warmer, drier summers, wetter autumns and winters, higher risks from drought, wind and flood, increased risks of pests and diseases, and higher growth from increased CO_2 levels. The warmer climate may favour some broadleaved trees in the north whilst making conditions too dry for others, such as beech, in the south and in marginal areas. The composition of our current woods will change as some species gradually gain advantage over others under the emerging conditions. Catastrophic events such as storms and fires will also reshape our woods.

Helping our existing woods to adapt to a changing climate is tricky, both because we are unsure about the future climate and because woods take decades to grow and change. The range of species in our woods is narrow: just 5 conifer species account for 88 per cent of softwood forests (Sitka spruce, Scots pine, larches, lodgepole pine, Norway spruce), and 5 species of hardwood make up 61 per cent of broadleaf woodland (birch, oak, ash, sycamore, beech). So there are obvious opportunities for diversifying species, age and structure, especially when restocking. Other useful steps include: relieving other stresses, such as pollution, invasive species and over-grazing; ensuring good tree health and vitality; buffering and linking woods where possible to increase their core area.

Good management of our existing forests can also mitigate climate breakdown by conserving the huge stocks of carbon in wood and soils, so preventing deforestation is just as urgent as halting fossil-fuel use. Research by the ecologist Dr Thomas Crowther has provided a more accurate measure of the carbon in the world's soils and forests. Management of these carbon stores both above and below ground can have huge impacts on our atmosphere. Increasing forest cover worldwide on marginal land by around one third could outstrip human greenhouse gas emissions whilst providing many other benefits as well. Dr Crowther goes on to suggest that planting trees on an epic scale would be 'overwhelmingly more powerful than all of the other climate-change solutions proposed'. About 1 trillion trees would be required, costing some $300 billion.

Well-managed forests yield wood products, from planks to panelboards, which can lock up carbon for decades. Using wood products for building has far lower energy consumption and carbon footprint than steel, brick and concrete. Once built, timber makes an excellent insulator, saving further energy over the lifetime of the building. Beyond these immediate considerations, climate breakdown is forcing us to reconsider what trees and woods are for. We have always thought of them primarily as providers of fuel and timber, places to graze animals, useful shelter from the elements. But now, as we find ourselves in a massively depleted world facing disruption of its climate dynamics, woods are being increasingly recognised for other vital functions, such as carbon storage and sequestration; moderators of water cycles, air quality and temperatures; stabilisers of landscapes; refugia for wildlife. Indeed, these contributions may be more important than traditional uses in the decades ahead.

DUTCH ELM DISEASE 1972
Dutch Elm Disease kills many elm woods and eliminates most hedgerow elms. Forty years later, the geographical distribution of elms is almost unaltered, but big elms are abundant only in Huntingdonshire, Cambridgeshire woodland, east Sussex, parts of Scotland and the Isles of Scilly.

Responding to tree disease

Major incidents of tree disease, like Dutch Elm, used to be occasional but are becoming more frequent. This is partly caused by the increase in global trade of live plants for instant landscaping, with unwelcome organisms arriving in the soil

The globalisation of tree disease: ash dieback (*top left*) is characterised by diamond-shaped lesions on the trunks of infected plants and dieback of the foliage. The micro-moth *Cameraria ohridella*, which mines the leaves of the horse chestnut tree (*top right*), is said to be from around the city of Ohrid in the Republic of Macedonia, where the horse chestnut itself originated. Bleeding black cankers on an oak (*middle left*) is associated with Acute Oak Decline. Emerald Ash Borer (*middle right*) make multiple tunnels through the phloem, killing the tree at least to ground level. It is exterminating ash across the United States and could soon arrive in the UK. Oak Mildew, *Microsphæra alphitoides* (*bottom left*), was introduced to the UK from North America c.1900. The Elm Zigzag Sawfly (bottom right), *Aproceros leucopoda*, has now been confirmed in Britain following a rapid expansion across Europe from eastern Asia.

Like bleached coral, the leafless branches of dead ash trees reveal the devastating effects of ash dieback in this mixed woodland in Kent. Photograph courtesy of Kent Downs AONB.

of potted plants, or on the bark; and partly caused by the massive increase in all forms of global movements from freight containers to vehicles. Some organisms are windblown. Climate change may also play a role by making our conditions more suitable for migrating pests and diseases.

Ash dieback is the latest major threat and has caused widespread grief amongst tree-lovers. The threat of loss hangs over ash, Yggdrasil, Tree of Life. The disease appears to have got here both in infected nursery stock and 'on the wind' from Continental Europe, and is now present throughout most of Britain. It is widespread on the Continent and has been damaging ash trees there since the 1990s. The disease seems to have originated in Asia, where it co-exists with Asian species of ash and is not considered a problem. But taken out of its evolutionary context and transported to Europe, where our ash has no resistance, it has wreaked ecological havoc.

It was first observed in the UK in 2012, although subsequent research found sites where it has been present since at least 2005. The cost of this calamity could total some £15 billion from felling costs, loss of timber and also the loss of all the other things ash trees provide, such as clean air and water and carbon storage.

At the moment, ash makes up about 12 per cent of broadleaved woodland, while outside woods ash is the most common large tree, successful as an individual tree or in groups in hedgerows, on railway embankments and growing vigorously in the gaps of the humanscape. So far, the experience from Denmark and Lithuania is that about 1 per cent of ash is resistant to the disease.

The Tree Council has collated information for homeowners, the general public and has also produced an Action Plan Toolkit to help local authorities prepare their own Ash Dieback Action Plan. Elsewhere around the UK, there are different examples of people getting together to take positive steps and seek out solutions to the spread of ash disease. The Kent Downs AONB ran the Ash Project between 2017 and 2018 to celebrate the county's commonest tree (*see* page 96). The Devon Ash Dieback Resilience Forum are monitoring the impact of the dieback – it is estimated that there are nearly half a million ash trees beside Devon's roads and 11,000 hectares of woodland is ash-dominated in the county. In neighbouring Dorset, the Springhead Trust collaborated with the Ancient Tree Forum to curate the Ashscape Project, a series of public events that celebrated the history and diversity of ash trees. The sound artist Adrian Newton created a soundscape from the internal gurgling sounds of an ash tree, leading to the performance of a song cycle written by Karen Wimhurst lamenting our beloved ash:

> You have been with us from the beginning.
> Stay!
> Stay with us forever!
> Ash our Tree of Life!

There has, however, been more promising news recently. Researchers have identified some disease-resistant genes and this could lead to breeding a new population of ash trees. Also, a study in north-east France found that although all ash trees acquired the disease, isolated trees were far more healthy than dense stands of ash. So hedgerow trees and open canopies fared better, especially where temperatures were higher, as the pathogen cannot survive above 35 degrees C.

ASH DIEBACK 2012
Ash disease is caused by the microscopic fungus Hymenoscyphus fraxineus that inhabits leaves and twigs, damaging them by making a chemical called viridiol that is toxic to ash

Dealing with pests

Although grey squirrels do not pose an existential threat to trees in the way that ash dieback does, they are considered to be the single greatest threat to growing quality broadleaves in much of Britain. They are particularly drawn to the smooth bark of trees in their teenage years or twenties, which they strip off to reach the juicy sap below in springtime. This stunts and disfigures the tree, ruins its timber quality and can undermine landowners' commitments to woodland management and planting.

Culling grey squirrels is a difficult task, and a tougher approach would not be supported by the public, although replacing the alien grey squirrels with our native red squirrels might just be both possible and acceptable. But how do we go about doing that? Red squirrels do not cause significant damage to trees, but they are currently out-competed by grey squirrels, which also spread squirrel pox to the reds (whilst remaining unaffected themselves). However, there is fascinating recent research about the effect of pine martens (another native species) on grey squirrels. In Ireland, for example, they have found that the pine martens disrupt the feeding and breeding of greys, reducing their numbers, which allows the native red squirrels to return to the forest. Pine-marten-introduction trials have now begun in the Forest of Dean.

Deer are also a major constraint on tree growth in Britain,

Pine martens (*Martes martes*) are shy members of the weasel family and are about the size of a domestic cat. Native to Britain, they have been driven back to the wilds of Scotland and Wales. In recent years there has been growing interest in bringing these predators back to more of Britain's forests, to restore a more balanced ecosystem.

Among the innovative pinewood regeneration and conservation projects in the Scottish Highlands is Project Wolf, which employed 'human wolves' to patrol the woodlands in Dundreggan between dusk and dawn. The walkers disturbed deer, discouraging them from eating young seedlings, allowing the next generation of trees to flourish. Photograph by Lisa Marley, from her documentary about Project Wolf.

though their impact does vary across the UK. Deer browse the growing tips of young trees, keeping them forever ankle-high and suppressing the next generation of trees from developing.

The deer population is thought to be at its highest level for 1,000 years, with numbers having doubled in the last 20 years. They have no natural predators in Britain any more, they benefit from mild winters and winter arable crops and, ironically, greater woodland cover. Like grey squirrels, people love to see deer in the countryside, often unaware of the problems they cause. But if we want a land with more trees and woods, we need to confront the issue of deer, decide what our priorities are and find a more natural balance.

These are just some of the challenges and threats to trees today. Ted Green (founder of the Ancient Tree Forum) goes further, arguing that as well as specific pests and disease, trees are under stress from a wide and subtle 'web of causation', including vehicle pollution, carbon dioxide, ozone, ultraviolet light and pesticides, while below the ground the essential mycorrhizae are increasingly compromised by soil disturbance and pollution from modern farming. Trees respond to this barrage of stress by slowly withdrawing vitality from their extremities and hunkering down to their core – a process known as 'dieback'.

Taking a cut

Given the challenges ahead, any vision for forestry must look after the trees and woods already growing. For forestry, this means sustainable forest management, which has been at the heart of UK policy for 20 years. The public forest estate accounts for 27 per cent of our UK forest, managed by the four state forestry services, and all of this is in various schemes of certified sustainable management. The rest of the UK's forest is in private hands, and only about half of this is officially managed. But can't we just leave trees and woods be? Why does nature need to be managed anyway?

Here we come face to face with a real cultural, even ethical, issue: if trees are so great why are we even talking about cutting them down? Shouldn't we leave them in the ground and find alternative materials to timber? And why do we talk about conserving ancient woods and hedges? Can't they cope without us? When is it right to intervene in nature? When is it right to cut down a tree?

The answer to all these questions is, it depends. . .

It depends on what tree, where it is, how it is done. We need the widest possible range of tree-care ideas and techniques, from non-intervention to occasional tweaking, from frequent small cuts to occasional bigger cuts to constant harvesting.

An ancient ash in a hedgerow with hollow trunk and stag head does not need any cutting at all, it just needs to be left alone, not ploughed nearby, not sprayed, not tidied up. An ancient wood on wet soils might also be best left to nature, allowing trees to grow old, fall down and be replaced by a new generation. A coppice wood of hazel or sweet chestnut, on the other hand, is a traditional management system practised over centuries and frequent cutting might well be the best strategy to retain its unique flora and fauna, which is dependent on periodic flooding with sunlight.

What about ancient oakwoods – how can it ever be right to fell them? The woods that have survived to this day have probably either proved themselves as useful for timber, or proved to be so difficult to work or convert to agriculture that they have been left alone. As Oliver Rackham remarked: once felled, trees regenerate themselves, either as coppice or by seed. Useful

Felled oak in a sweet-chestnut coppice, East Sussex. Chestnut coppice needs abundant sunlight to grow well, and too many overstorey trees stunt its growth. Here an oak has been felled to favour the coppice in the next rotation. The standing oak pictured has been retained for species and structural diversity.

woods will have been felled and restocked many times over the centuries, continuing the cycle. The woods on difficult ground would probably be best left alone. Yet woods are dynamic living communities which change over time of their own accord. So even if we do nothing, we are effectively committing the wood to a certain kind of change – one where the trees grow bigger,

RESTORATION

Fingle Woods in Devon was bought by the National Trust and the Woodland Trust in 2013. Their aim was to begin restoring this Plantation on an Ancient Woodland Site (PAWS), a process that could take at least 100 years.

PAWS like Fingle Woods can often still have the unique ground flora, undisturbed forest soils, ancient trees, and archaeology such as woodbanks. With careful and patient work, it is possible to gradually remove the densely shading conifers and encourage the native species to return.

The steepsided valleys of the River Teign contain unique soil and wildlife communities that have taken centuries to develop, but have been degraded by the plantation at Fingle Woods. The soils in the wood were already depleted after a thousand years of coppicing, but it is the conifer species planted in the twentieth century that have created extremely acid conditions and soil loss – when it rains heavily, flushes of acidity are found in the surrounding watercourses.

Protection of soils and water are important long-term aims for the restoration of Fingle Woods. But before restoration work could begin at Fingle, every forest nook and rocky ridge was studied to identify the ancient woodland remnants and ensure its unique qualities would be protected. Starting at the most run-down areas first, invasive plants were removed and rare species protected. Over time, the dense conifers will be carefully thinned so the sun can fall on the forest floor and reinvigorate life.

This approach to the restoration of Fingle is called 'Continuous Cover Forestry' (CCF). Unlike clearfelling, where a whole stand of trees is felled at maturity and replanted, the CCF approach maintains forest cover during felling and restocking.

'Replanted woods, or "Plantations on Ancient Woodland Sites" (PAWS for short), can often still retain the unique ground flora, undisturbed forest soils, ancient trees, and archaeology such as woodbanks.'

This means felling in 'coups' (sections of up to half a hectare) or selecting small groups of trees and even single trees for removal. The remaining forest protects the felled area, reducing exposure to wind, drought and sun, whilst maintaining forest conditions of humidity, mycorrhizal associations and shelter. Seed from surrounding trees can also help regenerate the felled area naturally.

The dominant conifer, Douglas fir, regenerates well on the steep valley sides and in the shallow acid soils. When it is well thinned its relatively 'light' canopy accommodates the development of a semi-natural ground flora, understorey and an increasing broadleaf canopy. The success of the Fingle Woods restoration will depend on how well this ancient soil structure has been preserved.

PAWS Restoration was pioneered by the Woodland Trust in 2002, backed by the Forestry Commission. The Woodland Trust had spotted that a whole cohort of post-war plantations on ancient woodland sites would soon be reaching maturity (planted in the 1960s and beginning to mature around 2000). The anticipated felling and restocking of these sites offered a unique opportunity for change: the price of conifer timber was fairly low so there was only minimal income foregone from converting 'economic' conifers to 'uneconomic' broadleaves.

The Woodland Trust argued that conifers should be gradually removed and native trees restored. At first viewed with scepticism by the forestry community, PAWS Restoration has now become an accepted and widely practised idea, with grants from the Forestry Commission (continued under the Countryside Stewardship scheme) to offset the costs of installing tracks for harvesting, uneconomic thinning and the clearing of rhododendron.

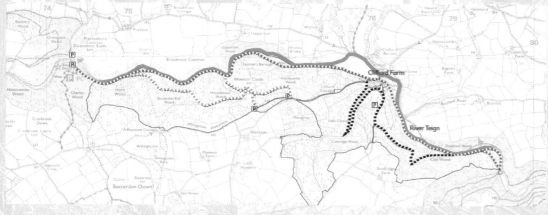

FINGLE WOODS: finglewoods.org.uk

Prime Coppice is a 21-hectare ancient wood in the Marshwood Vale, Dorset. Since 2011 the owners have introduced sustainable management: restoring coppice, thinning neglected areas, restoring an area of wood pasture, managing the woodland edge for biodiversity, restoring woodland ponds and increasing the structural diversity in the wood. They also use sympathetic management practices such as horse extraction of timber.

the wood becomes denser and light is steadily excluded.

It is always a weighty decision to fell a century-old oak, and we really have to be confident that we are working sustainably. To do this, foresters use simple measurements to calculate the growth of trees in a forest, so as to work out how much increment they are putting on each year – literally the sum total of all those annual rings. From this they calculate how much can be harvested in any given period (usually ten years for an oak stand), and then choose the trees to fulfil the quota, taking care to leave enough for the forest to grow as well. Then there are other considerations in the forest: spacing, the form of the tree, quality of the stem, wildlife habitats. So making the final decision of what tree to fell is as much an art as a science.

Conifer forests planted explicitly for timber are obvious candidates for cutting down, but even here we have to consider how best to do it. Many of the post-war pure conifer plantations have reached the end of their economic rotation and are being felled and restocked. They were often planted with little regard to existing landforms and features, so felling offers an opportunity to restructure them to fit better into the landscape and restore valuable streams, bogs, crags and remnants of native trees, such as rowan, birch and alder. This is now national policy. Where conifers are planted over existing ancient woods (known as Plantations on Ancient Woodland

SUSTAINABLE MANAGEMENT
OF NEW AND EXISTING FORESTS

EXISTING FORESTS

Forest health must come first - promote a healthy forest ecology, tread carefully, foster diversity, build resilience.

Timber harvesting must be appropriate and not threaten other values - in ancient or SSSI woodland ensure that

conservation comes first. That may mean little or no harvesting.

Habitats must be restored - PAWS must be restored, streams should have dense shade removed, historical blanket planting should be restructured to respect natural diversity.

Forest conditions must be made resilient - diversify monocultures, restructure even-age plantations.

Avoid large clearfells and loss of forest conditions - we must keep the overall forest structure as intact as possible to retain the shelter, shade, humidity, nutrients, water, soil and the mycorrhizal safety net.

NEW FORESTS

Allow natural regeneration where possible - let nature take its course. Rewilding can produce surprising and exciting landscapes.

If planting, take great care over site selection - we need good arable land for food, so low-grade agricultural land may be more suitable for extensive plantations, or reclaimed ex-industrial land.

Make suitable adaptations to climate change - consider more resilient mixed stands, source some seed from more southerly origins.

More productive conifers and more productive hardwoods are required to meet our needs for timber and forest products.

Plant mixtures of fast- and slow-growing trees, light- and shade-loving trees to make best use of resources, plus trees for soil improvement. We also need more planting for shelter, shade, amenity, flood control, health and wellbeing, fruits and nuts carefully designed for maximum benefit.

Develop a strategic network of semi-natural habitats to improve the ecological functioning of our landscapes.

Restructuring even-age monoculture plantations into nature-based diverse stands. *Top*: Beech with Douglas fir and larch. *Bottom*: Spruce with beech and sycamore. Image courtesy of J. B. Larsen.

Sites, or PAWS) there is a real urgency to address the threat of shade to the remnant flora (*see* pages 144–145). We need not have scruples about felling some of these trees.

At the busier end of the spectrum there are energy 'crops' that require constant harvesting such as willow or hazel coppice, which are cut every few years for chipping and feeding into the biomass boilers.

Of course, managing woods can also maintain a diversity of habitats, from dense, dark, humid woods through regularly cut coppice to open wood pasture. Not every wood needs to have great habitat diversity, but there should be diversity at the landscape scale – something of everything appropriate to the local conditions. Our woods have become too small and fragmented for a diversity of habitats to occur naturally, so we need to intervene to create them.

Because we use a lot of timber in our daily lives, we must take responsibility for where it comes from and how it grows. Taking responsibility means planting more productive conifer forests and felling trees for our reasonable needs. We need more woods along all points of the spectrum of productivity, from conservation woods left to evolve naturally, through small woods worked by local people, right up to plantations worked on an industrial scale.

The abundant forest

Our peculiar forest history can distort our view of forestry. Most of our productive woods have been planted on bare land in the last century, so forestry can appear to be a linear process, from hillside to plantation to clearfell, more like an agricultural crop than a long-standing forest undergoing cycles of harvesting. Given the land available, the trees that can grow in these places (exotic conifers) and the timber objectives, the industrial plantation system, modelled on German forest science, was thought to be the most efficient way to proceed.

Where there are deeper soils, there is a greater choice of species and a wider variety of objectives for the wood, including conservation and biodiversity, recreation and landscape. There are also more choices in the way these woods are managed: stands of trees can be steadily improved over the decades by thinning to produce fewer but finer trees at the end of the rotation, and the 'thinnings' provide an income from woodfuel and timber in the meantime.

Careful selection of trees for felling in small groups, or even singly, maintains stable forest conditions for protection, humidity and weed suppression. This approach to managing woodland (Continuous Cover Forestry) aims to maintain the integrity of the stand whilst removing trees on a regular cycle, rather than by clearfelling at the end of rotation. The gaps created by cutting are restocked by natural regeneration and/ or planting.

Current thinking in forestry is questioning the monocultural planting and clearfelling methods practised in the plantation. All forests need to become more resilient in order to withstand and recover from shocks of climate disruption and an increase in pests and diseases. Forest resilience can be improved through the diversity of trees and other forest species, genetic diversity within

Natural regeneration, as in this oak stand in Gloucestershire, can be more desirable than planting because it conserves local genotypes, creates more diverse woods and gives assurance that species are suited to the site. Natural regeneration can be used both for restocking existing woods, and for expanding woods onto adjacent land.

each tree species, functioning soils and structural diversity of the stands. Mycorrhizal fungi are particularly helpful in supporting the forest under stress, while sequestering carbon in the soil.

When considering restocking a felled area or planting a new wood, it is important to consider carefully which species to use and be sure of the provenance of seeds and saplings. Ancient woods will require mostly local native seed, but some additional seed from more southerly, warmer countries would be helpful in view of climate change. Newer woods or 'secondary woods' need not be so constrained and could look at a higher proportion of alternative species and provenances to plant.

There has been a native versus non-native species debate about trees for years. It arises because our islands were cut off from the European Continent about 8,000 years ago, leaving us with a relatively impoverished 'native' flora and fauna. Nevertheless, our semi-natural habitats have evolved over the millennia to create distinctive natural assemblages, and these are often the objects of conservation action.

Woods are not just about wood: we can also harvest food, medicines and other non-timber forest products from the trees. There are examples of extraordinarily productive tree-based growing systems, such as this Forest Garden in Dartington, Devon, developed by Martin Crawford at the Agroforestry Research Trust. The secret is to emulate the many layers of the forest to create a self-regulating system where all you have to do is harvest. Photograph courtesy of Martin Crawford.

Moor Trees collects thousands of local tree seeds for growing in its community tree nursery. It then plants out the saplings on private and public land with the aim of restoring native woodland to Dartmoor.

Have you heard of the wild service tree (*Sorbus torminalis*)? The fruits, also known as chequers, are said to taste like dates and were given to children as sweets. They can be made into an alcoholic drink and it is thought they influenced the naming of Chequers Inns, although it is unclear which came first – the name of the fruit or the inns. The tree is also an indicator of ancient woods, and the timber is highly prized. It is best planted as small groups or scattered individual trees, such as in this pasture near Vienna, Austria. Photograph by Christopher Guest.

The International Union for Conservation of Nature requires a species to have been growing here since at least 1500 before we can call it 'native'. However, this definition doesn't recognise the contribution that non-natives make to Britain's biodiversity and the character of particular places. Nor does it consider the impact of climate disruption or the advent of new disease as one species after another becomes threatened: first elm, now ash, maybe oak next?

Beech trees were heavily affected by the Great Storm of 1987, and every subsequent storm sees further losses of veteran beeches. As weather becomes more extreme, both wetter and windier and hotter and drier, native beech trees may become unsuitable for their natural habitat in the south-east of England. It would be unwise to dismiss non-native species as contributors to conservation.

Our ecosystems are undergoing disruption on a scale previously unseen for millennia. As climate and land-use changes, there will be winners and losers amongst the trees and other species. We

Left: Trial plantation of eucalyptus in Devon. Could this be a woodfuel crop of the future?

Below: As we approach a more Mediterranean climate, species such as olive could become more common, as they are in this Devon garden designed by Conrad Batten.

can help struggling species in some places and embrace other lesser-known natives like the wild service tree, while welcoming non-native tree species, including sycamore, sweet chestnut and walnut, in others. We need to keep an open mind and respond creatively to the changing world.

Restocking and new planting could make more use of mixtures. The monocultural plantation tends to use a narrow range of a site's resources of light, nutrients and soil. Jonathan Spencer, a former ecologist at the Forestry Commission, suggests planting mixtures: fast-growing species with slower emergent trees, understorey trees that make use of the lower light levels, and trees that improve the soil. A conifer main crop, for example, might include birch for early cover and soil improvement, Douglas fir as the emergent timber tree, western red cedar as a shade-tolerant understorey and some alder for nitrogen fixation. A broadleaf mix might fulfil these roles with aspen, oak, hornbeam or lime, plus alder.

Forest stewardship

If we are to intervene in woods and natural processes, we should only do so after deep consideration of the impacts, on the wood itself and on the wider web of interconnected life. Over the last 20 years, these considerations have become codified in forestry standards and stewardship schemes.

In the UK, post-war forest expansion was causing public concern by the 1970s and 1980s, not simply because of the blanketing of upland habitats and old woodland sites with conifer plantations, but also because of the tax regime that allowed the super-rich to avoid taxes. So during the 1990s, bridges were built between business, environmental and social NGOs, leading to what is known as the UK Forestry Standard: 'the government's approach to sustainable forestry'. This underpins what is understood as acceptable and unacceptable forestry practice, and people in the forestry sector must comply with these rules in order to receive Forestry Commission grants.

At the same time, in response to worldwide 'accelerating deforestation, environmental degradation and social exclusion', an idea emerged to create a global, independent certification

COMMUNITY STEWARDSHIP

A community workshop in the Wyre Forest, exploring ideas in wood and collaboration, make a 'nest' from waste timber from the forest floor.

Wyre Forest is a 4500-hectare ancient woodland dominated by oak but also including species-rich meadows and orchards. The oak woodland has its origins in large-scale coppice for charcoal and other products needed for the industrial West Midlands. Over the last 80 years, the woodland has seen little active management – it was too immature to harvest during the Second World War, so it was abandoned.

The Wyre Community Land Trust is a social enterprise that undertakes a range of practical work in and around the Wyre Forest. They directly manage about 240 hectares of farmland, conservation land and woodland across this area for a range of partners and private landowners. They also have a herd of Dexter cattle for conservation grazing and work extensively with the local community.

With a team of permanent staff and volunteers, the Land Trust sustainably and economically manages a variety of habitats within the Wyre Forest landscape, from species-rich meadows to orchards, heathland and neglected ancient woods. Because there hasn't been much active management in the Wyre Forest, there has been a loss of local wood-processing capacity for mature broadleaved products, and therefore a loss of woodland economy associated with the forest.

This has meant they've had to start a new woodland business model, with a woodyard and sawmill that processes mostly lower-grade oak for woodfuel and other products. But there is also a need to invest in renovating the wood ahead of producing high-quality timber, which includes programmes of extensive thinning to reinvigorate regeneration while leaving the best timber trees to grow to reach their economic potential.

Their aim is to develop new ways to manage traditional and cherished landscapes. They want to find new economic and social drivers that can create the energy to manage landscapes outside of mainstream agriculture and forestry. This means bringing people back into the landscapes, supporting livelihoods and a thriving community, celebrating and understanding the place.

WYRE COMMUNITY LAND TRUST: wyreclt.org.uk
RUSKIN LAND: ruskinland.org.uk **STUDIO IN THE WOODS:** invisiblestudio.org

Timber stacks: logs and bars on the right and low-grade chipwood on the left.

scheme that could 'credibly identify well-managed forests as the sources of responsibly produced wood products'. The Rio Earth Summit of 1992 supported the idea, and it led to the founding of the Forest Stewardship Council (FSC) in 1993.

Certification covers much more than just the forestry operations. The FSC principles cover legal issues and use rights, community relations and workers' rights, environmental impacts and conservation, forest management and monitoring. The FSC standards are universal, applying equally in the rainforests of Borneo and the spruce plantations of Dumfries, and it is in those areas with a much richer forest culture that the wider impacts of forestry are particularly felt, for better and worse.

These standards have been filtered through the particular requirements of UK forestry to establish the UK Woodland Assurance Standard (UKWAS). Certification certainly does set the bar higher than national laws and codes of practice, in both environmental and social requirements. Many commercial organisations undertake certification as a necessary burden to acquire access to markets. For example, timber mills in the UK usually require 70 per cent of their stock to have come from certified sources, so the chances of selling your timber is greatly improved by having the certificate.

Although many charities, local authorities, small businesses and other organisations do not actually harvest or sell any timber, they can still adopt FSC certification because it expresses their green credentials. This book, for example, is printed on paper sourced from FSC certified forests. But who checks that forest owners or suppliers signed up to the certification programme are actually doing what they say?

Anybody taking part in forest stewardship is visited regularly by an auditor, who will not only check the condition of the forest itself, but also a range of office procedures and paperwork to ensure that licences are in place; any disputes are addressed; management plans are adequate, implemented and monitored; biodiversity is protected; the local community is consulted; and there is proper provision for health and safety and training.

Building with timber

William Bryant Logan, author and arborist, describes how 'people built their world out of wood for 10,000 years', from the dawn of civilisation till about 200 years ago. We have co-evolved with our woods, taking more than we give for sure, but it is still a dynamic partnership. Now building with wood is experiencing a renaissance in Britain.

We need a new vernacular architecture to reflect today's concerns, based on locally sourced and renewable materials, with

The Mess Building at Westonbirt Arboretum was designed by Invisible Studio and constructed entirely from timber grown and milled on-site with minimal processing, using building techniques pioneered in making the Caretaker's House at Hooke Park, Dorset. The project received a National RIBA Award in addition to three Regional RIBA Awards.

Construction of the two CLT buildings at Trafalgar Place in Elephant and Castle, London, took only six weeks and reduced the carbon impact of constructing 1800 m² of living space with traditional reinforced concrete. The timber used was spruce-sourced from FSC-certified forests in Austria. The project was designed by dRMM using engineering techniques developed in their Timber Studio. Photograph by Daniel Romero, courtesy of dRMM.

low-embedded energy and low-energy running requirements, resilient to the climate of the future, whilst remaining affordable. We need houses that lock up more carbon than they use in their production, and generate more energy than they consume in daily use. Wood is surely the material to deliver these benefits.

Wood can be used in many forms. It can be used substantially unchanged in the round as poles or square sawn as beams; it can be sawn into planks and studwork of any dimension; it can be sliced thinly and glued back together in several layers at right angles to make plywood and cross-laminated timber (CLT); it

TŶ UNNOS by Owen Griffiths, National Botanic Garden, Carmarthenshire, Wales, 2017

In Wales there is a tradition of *tŷ unnos* (one-night house), dating back several hundred years. It suggests that if you were able to build a house on common land, with a fire smoking out from the chimney, the land and house would be rightfully yours. The idea of a one-night house appears throughout the world, mostly as folklore but sometimes in customary and even statutory law.

In the spirit of *tŷ unnos,* the artist Owen Griffiths created a public performance and vernacular structure in collaboration with over 30 volunteers, staff and visitors of the National Botanic Garden of Wales. By weaving local tree stories and timber materials into his residency with Common Ground, the project also explores contemporary political issues of land and sustainability through the relationship between the trees and people in the Carmarthenshire landscape.

Watts Grove, the UK's first mid-rise CLT modular scheme, was built in 2019 by the Swan Housing Association. The CLT modular homes were delivered to the site in Tower Hamlets, London, complete with kitchens, bathrooms and windows.

can be sawn in small dimensions, glued together lengthways and finger-jointed to make glued laminated beams (glulam); it can be shaved into flakes and glued back together as oriented strand board (OSB); or completely mashed up and stuck together to make medium-density fibreboard (MDF).

Building a traditional masonry house typically creates 65 tonnes of CO_2 emissions. Furthermore, houses built today have as little as 50 years' life expectancy. A timber house, however, can enjoy 200 years of use. Once built, a contemporary wooden house can also be much cheaper to run. A small electric heater powered by renewable energy should be enough for such a well-insulated home. At the end of its (long) life, wooden houses can be decommissioned with some parts being re-used, others recycled and waste wood burnt for energy.

Unlike bricks and mortar, where a house has to be built up layer upon layer on-site, timber frames and panels can be fabricated off-site in the workshop, then assembled on-site in a fraction of the time – as little as three days for a three-bed house. This makes construction quicker, safer and more flexible. Scotland is leading the way in this field with some 75 per cent of new-builds using timber frames, compared with only 15 per cent in England and Wales, a difference which only reflects a

WORKING IN WOOD

Elwy Working Woods (EWW) in Abergele, on the north coast of Wales, was established as a co-operative in 2009 – just about anybody can become a member, so long as they recognise the value of trees and woods to the local economy and a sustainable future.

There are 20 members at the moment, most of them under 30 years old: a mixture of forestry contractors, carpenters, joiners and timber-framers. As a co-operative, EWW exists primarily for their benefit: to safeguard jobs, create new skills and stimulate opportunities, to use shared networks, timber, insurance, machinery, tools and workshop space. For all this, each person pays a membership fee and the co-op charges an additional admin fee to cover overheads, which applies to sales of members' goods and services.

Because EWW is a social enterprise, it can give priority to the social and environmental dimension of their work, not just the profitability, with a particularly strong focus on rural job creation and investing in the sustainable management of woods. EWW owns and looks after about 100 acres of mixed broadleaf and conifer, but has extended its management work across other local woodlands over the last five years, including some mature woods on local farms and estates.

Over the years, EWW members have built a large variety of structures, from log-sheds and staircases to garages and three-bedroom houses. They also sell firewood, furniture, gates, handmade pieces from the turnery, alongside running a number of training programmes and consulting the government on upland planting programmes and affordable timber-frame housing in Wales.

EWW is also hoping to find ways to reduce the costs of living for young forestry workers, particularly in housing: they want to find ways of building that is both locally sourced and affordable. This is something facing communities and local planners all over the UK. Can affordable homes be low-carbon homes? And what role can local wood and other materials play in solving the problem? Surely, members of social enterprises like EWW will play a role in exploring these important questions.

Legal & General have built a factory at Sherburn-in-Elmet near Leeds to make their precision-engineered modular homes using cross-laminated timber (CLT). They aim to address our housing crisis with 'sustainable, durable, modern materials and proven technology.' Photograph by Nick Sievewright, kindly supplied by Footprint Photography.

cultural attitude apparently. In Yorkshire, Citu have developed a wooden house that sequesters 23 tonnes of CO_2 emissions and is built from timber sourced – over 75 per cent – from forests in UK and Ireland, with the engineered CLT timber made from softwood grown in Sweden and Germany.

The high strength-to-weight ratio of wood means that architects and developers are now aspiring to build high-rise structures using 'mass timber' – meaning the primary load-bearing structure is timber or engineered wood. The 'Stadthaus' in Hackney, London, dramatically raised the bar for timber buildings in 2008. Built mostly from cross-laminated timber, at nine storeys it was then the tallest residential timber building in the world. Timber technology has accelerated rapidly and in British Colombia, Canada, an eighteen-storey timber-framed building was built in three weeks.

Lots of wood is used in such buildings, which effectively locks up the carbon for decades to come. The UK government's Committee on Climate Change agrees there is a significant role for timber: 'There is potential to substantially increase the use of timber in construction in the UK. This will provide a low-cost route to Green House Gas (GHG) abatement through to 2050'.

The argument for wood in construction becomes even more

compelling if we factor in the social cost of carbon – this is the estimated cost of the damage caused by every tonne of carbon emitted to the atmosphere. These costs may be an order of magnitude higher than first thought by governments and could be some £325 per tonne. As wood generates a 'social benefit' as a carbon store, it becomes cheaper than concrete and steel, which both have high GHG production emissions.

Nationally, we currently produce from our own forests about one third of the sawn timber we use in construction and over half of the wood panels; the rest is imported. More timber could be squeezed from our own forests and significant increases could come from large-scale afforestation, but this will take decades to mature. Improvements in grading could also make more homegrown timber available, by using a wider range of species and by using lower-specification timbers for lower-grade uses.

Woodfuel

Sitting round the bonfire feeling the sharp heat on your cheeks, the wood letting go of all that sunlight it has soaked up over the previous summers, the heat of the sun held in wood, now shining back out again... Burning wood for heat is ancient, and nobody can resist gazing into a flickering flame. Yet burning wood is getting complicated. Some see it as carbon neutral, because the burnt wood is releasing carbon that has *already* been absorbed during a tree's life, and if more fuel is grown in well-managed forests, the new trees will soak up carbon again in a matter of years. So burning and growing woodfuel works with the carbon already in our atmosphere, and is preferable to digging up much older carbon in the form of coal, oil or gas, which would otherwise stay out of circulation. But burning wood does still release carbon dioxide into the atmosphere at a time when we should be emitting less.

Earth's carbon cycle is way off balance: excessive fossil carbon has been released into the atmosphere over the last 250 years, while deforestation has reduced carbon sequestration. There is a strong and clear argument for trees having a major role in establishing a low-carbon future, maintaining and building carbon stocks in forests and soils, sucking carbon out of the

The Wood Chip Barn, located at the Architectural Association's woodland campus at Hooke Park in Dorset, provides long-term storage to fuel the biomass boiler that heats the workshops, accommodation and learning spaces. The barn's arching structure is formed from forked beech-tree components directly sourced from the surrounding woodland. Photograph by Graham Shackleton.

atmosphere and storing it in living wood and soils, and offering timber as an alternative construction material. But what role will wood play in replacing fossil fuels with renewable biofuels?

Over the last twenty years the European Union and the UK government have used different incentives to encourage people to invest more in renewable energy, including biomass and firewood. All this has had a huge impact on woods in the UK since the early 2000s. Before then, firewood was a cheap by-product of other works in the forest. As demand and prices rose, however, cutting firewood became an end in itself and a very useful market for the vast amounts of small, low-grade hardwood from our mixed broadleaved woods. Suddenly, small woods became more economically viable and started being managed again, paid for by firewood orders. Neglected stands could again be regenerated,

Woodland Social Enterprises process firewood in a variety of ways, from using handtools like bow saws and axes to training themselves up for chainsaw use or log-splitting by machine. But even those who do not want to cut down trees or operate chainsaws can collect and stack by hand. And the results are just the same: a load of logs to take home and burn! Photograph by Axewoods.

access improved, thinning undertaken at the right time and quality trees secured for the future.

A rising demand for firewood and an abundance of neglected woods has enabled the growth of Woodland Social Enterprises (*see* pages 122–127), which offer opportunities for a wide range of skills, interests and abilities. There are innovative firewood schemes all over the country, such as the 'wood allotments' at Spud Wood in Cheshire and the Dartmoor Woodfuel Co-operative; the 'log banks' of Axewoods Co-operative in east Devon and the Silverdale District Woodbank, which are both volunteer groups also engaged with woodland management and tackling fuel poverty; the Leeds Coppice Workers co-operative which aims to create jobs, produce ethically sourced firewood and promote sustainable woodland management.

However, when badly managed, firewood can turn out the opposite of eco-friendly, with high levels of toxic emissions and particulates. The problem has grown in recent years, largely because poor-quality firewood is being burnt inefficiently on

The Silverdale District Woodbank works closely with the Arnside and Silverdale AONB, Woodland Trust, Natural England and other landowners in the area to nurture closer relationships between local woods, people and wildlife. In return for helping manage these woods, members share the timber generated to take as firewood or coppice craft material.

open fires in residential areas. It can take up to two years of air-drying for a fresh log with 50 per cent moisture content to dry down to 20 per cent, although kiln drying is quicker. But firewood that hasn't been dried properly exacerbates local air pollution, smouldering as it boils off the embodied water and emitting far more particulate matter than drier firewood. In response, an organisation called Woodsure has started certifying suppliers of woodfuel and recommends that we use 'Ready to Burn' wood with low moisture content.

Efficient burning is also essential to make best use of the firewood and minimise pollution. Wood-burning stoves have become popular in recent years, with one million stoves selling from 2010 to 2015. These are generally much more efficient than open fires, with the most advanced modern stoves performing significantly better on particulate emissions: a modern stove burning dry wood can reduce emissions by over 80 per cent compared to wetter wood on an open fire. We need to raise the bar on burning firewood – dry wood burnt in efficient stoves outside of city centres – or curtail our use.

But unless you live off-grid, burning firewood in a wood stove is probably not the only way you cook, heat water or warm your home. If you do use wood as a primary source of heat for your home or business, you are more than likely using a small or medium-sized wood pellet stove. These 'biomass' boilers use woodchip or wood pellets delivered in bulk, and are commonly installed to heat homes, business premises, clusters of buildings and 'district' community facilities. At the industrial end of the scale there are power stations such as Drax, importing (mainly from the United States) over 6 million tonnes of wood pellets and producing about 34 terawatt hours of energy every year – this is more than half of all the biomass energy generated in the UK, from one power station.

As with firewood, using biomass woodfuel is problematic – some see it as a way to wean ourselves off fossil fuels and reduce greenhouse gas emissions, while others see it as reckless incineration of valuable habitat and a driver of increased emissions. Indeed, a rigorous analysis of biomass published by the UK Committee on Climate Change warned that unless the production and use of biomass is low-carbon, sustainable and subject to strict governance, there are risks that biomass could be 'worse for the climate than using fossil fuels'.

So how can we ensure that using woody biomass for heating (at a local scale) and energy production (on an industrial scale) is a force for good? By maintaining high carbon stocks in the forests, harvesting carefully and applying a hierarchy of use to anything we harvest.

Old-growth forests and ancient wood (at home and abroad), with high carbon stocks, must not be cleared and replaced with plantations for biomass because it will result in a net loss of carbon, not to mention the damage to the forest ecosystem. Bringing neglected younger woods into active management can increase carbon sequestration, improve tree resilience and enhance the biodiversity of a woodland, but management must

Industrial biomass: construction of the biomass unloading and storage facility at Drax began in March 2009. It is a steel structure that accommodates up to 75,000 tonnes of biomass wood pellets. Its completion in June 2010 marked the beginning of the co-firing of wood and coal project at the plant. Photograph courtesy of the Spencer Group and Drax.

be sustainable: all harvested trees must be swiftly replaced, by replanting, natural regeneration, coppice regrowth, or, after thinning, by increased growth by the remaining trees. Soil disturbance must also be minimised during harvesting and restocking to retain the precious soil carbon, often several times higher than the carbon in the trees.

Another way to generate woody biomass is by planting short rotation coppice of willow, poplar or miscanthus (elephant grass) on low-grade pasture. As well as yielding a crop every few years, these biomass crops can also increase soil carbon, protect the land from erosion and moderate water flows. Meeting the current demands for biomass by growing it ourselves sounds like a sensible idea. But to keep the hoppers at Drax and other power stations full, how much land would we need to allocate for fuel crops?

As part of the 'powering down' scenario towards a zero carbon Britain, the Centre for Alternative Technology suggests that one-quarter of the renewable energy generated in the UK could come from biomass, which would be used to produce biogas (to replace natural gas), synthetic hydrocarbon fuel and heat. To create this much energy would need 4.1 million hectares of energy crops and short rotation forestry of birch, alder and sycamore. The Committee on Climate Change isn't quite as ambitious, but they still suggest a central role for Bio-Energy with Carbon Capture and Storage (BECCS), including an extra 1 million hectares of biomass plantation. To put this in perspective: there are currently 3 million hectares of woodland in the UK.

There is a widespread political and cultural consensus that more trees can address the climate crisis. Yet there is very little in political manifestos, reports or in the media about our current and future demand for biomass. We clearly need to think through the role that energy crops will play, how and where they can be planted, engage with landowners who might want to embark on these land-use changes, and consider how they can best fit into the natural mosaic of the land to benefit wildlife.

We need to develop a 'hierarchy of use' for wood, starting with the fundamental premise that the best use of a tree is to leave it growing. If we do harvest trees, the best human use for timber would be in construction, because the building process stores carbon for the long-term while displacing the use of carbon-intensive steel and cement. Wood for fuel is somewhere near the bottom of the hierarchy.

Wood recycling

There is an alternative destination for wood other than burning at the end of its life: to be recycled and returned to use. Pioneered in Brighton and Hove by The Wood Store Social Enterprise, there is now a network of over 25 'Community Wood Recycling' centres in Britain. They collect wood waste from sites, such as pallets and demolition timber, and aim to re-use it as high up the waste hierarchy as possible.

The waste hierarchy starts with reducing the amount of waste produced; then re-using wood for the same purpose where possible; then recycling the wood into a different product; failing that, the wood can be burnt and the energy recovered; the last resort is landfill.

WOOD RECYCLING

Newcastle Wood Recycling was set up as a Community Interest Company in September 2014 to rescue and re-use waste timber, providing a more environmentally and socially responsible alternative to landfill or chipping in the region. They have transformed a previously disused council depot into a vibrant and creative workplace with an on-site shop where they sell wooden products made by volunteers and there is studio space for local creatives. Newcastle Wood Recycling is part of a network of Community Wood Recyclers, originally set up in Brighton in 1998.

The organisation offers a waste-wood-collection service – a great alternative to a skip. Wood collected is re-used or recycled in the most environmentally friendly way, and sold on for DIY material, as unique furniture and garden products or as firewood. The work is highly labour-intensive enabling the provision of valuable and exciting volunteering opportunities for local people – especially those marginalised by society, such as long-term unemployed, asylum seekers, refugees, people with disabilities, and young people not in education, employment or training.

With a strong work ethic and supportive community within the woodyard, the Newcastle Recycling Centre helps people develop themselves both personally and professionally. They train volunteers in woodwork and Health and Safety, and have established a supportive community within the woodyard, enabling volunteers to work and learn in a safe and inspiring environment.

NEWCASTLE WOOD RECYCLING CIC: welovewood.org
BRIGHTON & HOVE WOOD RECYCLING PROJECT: woodrecycling.org.uk

The Brighton and Hove Wood Recycling Project celebrates Brighton Pride at their Wood Store. A not-for-profit social enterprise, the project started in 1998 and was the first recycling scheme of its kind in the country. They collect waste timber for re-use and recycling. With hundreds of thousands of tonnes of wood sent to landfill across the UK every year, much more unwanted wood could be collected and re-used, creating opportunities for people to gain work experience and learn new skills at the same time.

The Brighton store sells sawn timber, posts, scaffold boards, sheets of ply, MDF and OSB; vintage floorboards and joists; furniture that they have made from reclaimed wood; firewood, kindling and charcoal.

In 2016 the centres collected over 17,000 tonnes of wood nationwide, nearly half of which was re-used and the rest recycled. To achieve this they provided training and workplaces for more than 660 people. The centres are social enterprises and have a strong commitment to creating jobs and training for local people, especially those who are marginalised from the workplace.

STARS 15 by Ellie Davies

Ellie has been working in UK forests for the past nine years, making work which explores the complex interrelationship between the landscape and the individual. She has won many awards for her images and was included in *Arboreal* (2016), Common Ground's collection of writing about trees, woods and people.

INTO A LAND OF TREES

FROSTY TWIGS, HALSDON, DOLTON, DEVON, C.1990, by James Ravilious

In 1986, Common Ground started work on Trees, Woods and the Green Man, a project which invited different artists, sculptors, photographers, illustrators, poets, cartoonists, playwrights and writers to explore the natural and cultural value of trees, and worked to deepen popular concern and practical caring for trees by publishing pamphlets, a newspaper called *PULP!* and several books, as well as commissioning plays and initiating art exhibitions at Tate Britain, the Natural History Museum and the Southbank Centre. During 1989 and 1990, Common Ground commissioned James Ravilious to photograph the orchards and woods of the West Country, and his extraordinary photographs continue to be exhibited nationwide.

Imagine these islands with large forests, small woods and a countryside dotted with trees, covering about a third of the land. Some of these forests are hard-working and productive, supplying timber for building, carpentry and heating our homes; other forests might emerge from the return of wild nature and native trees; others might be small community woods gently managed for wildlife and people, or planted to hold back flood waters; exhausted farmland could relax and welcome back its protective mantle of trees and scrub; each wood will make our land that bit more resilient to a turbulent world. All these woods and forests are stitched together by hedgerow corridors, wildflower meadows, floodplains and marshes, which encourage locally distinctive species and new natives.

Are we just dreaming? Is this sort of joined-up thinking possible, nationwide, county by county, region by region?

We need to restore the web of life – the plants, trees and animals and our place among them. This will require ambition and commitment: to call a truce in our conquest of nature, to restore where we can, to allow nature to lead the way. We need an 'NHS for nature' providing support and emergency treatment for the natural world. Trees and woods are an important part of that and can help rebuild our wider relationship with nature.

For centuries our forests have been destroyed in favour of alternative land-uses with more immediate economic value. So what if we come at this from the opposite direction? What if we decide what sort of landscape we want, including how much forest, then devise the economic forces to deliver it? What if, instead of the wooded landscape being pushed back by economic requirements, we could turn the tables and make the economy subordinate to our choices? What if we decide to re-weave our little bit of the web of life, starting with trees? What if, instead of following blind market forces, we hold a bold vision?

The state decided (that is to say 'we' decided) a hundred years ago that Britain needed more trees and set about the task with its own resources (via the Foresty Commission) and by devising supportive policies for the private sector. We have described the impressive but mixed results of this elsewhere in this book. Could we embark on a similar mission, but do it better this time?

The need could hardly be more urgent. The United Nations reports on biodiversity warn us that nature is deteriorating worldwide at an increasing rate, and that urgent and concerted efforts are required for transformative change. The web of life is unravelling before our eyes and we have to stop it.

More trees and woods

Much of this book argues that nature must have a greater role in our lives. By putting this thinking into practice, the obvious way we could encourage more trees and woods is simply to stop preventing their growth and allow natural regeneration to fill the land with trees. There are certainly places where this works well: in Scotland, for example, fences and other forms of deer control exclude the primary suppressors of trees (red deer and sheep) and enable 'new' forest to emerge from the heather.

The other approach is more familiar: planting trees ourselves. This may feel like a good thing to do, but it also perpetuates an interventionist attitude to nature, where *we* decide what happens and manipulate the land accordingly, controlling the species, location and crucially the speed at which trees become established. If we urgently want to produce more of our own quality timber, we need to plant certain species at certain densities for the best results. Likewise for our carbon targets: we can plant the trees best suited to hoovering up CO_2. However, there is always the danger of thinking we know best and the land is littered with examples of where we got it wrong.

A recent RSPB report reviewed the complicated interactions of trees with wildlife and carbon. It is not as simple as saying 'plant trees to sequester carbon', because it depends where you plant them, what trees, how long they grow, what happens to them if

and when they are felled, and what the alternatives are at every stage of this long journey. Similarly for wildlife – it depends on which trees where and how the wood develops. At every step there are choices – what sort of land for trees? Not deep peat or wildflower meadows because of the loss of carbon and existing wildlife respectively. What sort of trees? Conifers will hoover up carbon quicker, but oak and beech are longer-lived and hold the carbon for longer. The effect of each choice depends on the counter-factual scenario – what would have happened if the forest had been thinned, or the wood used for building or biofuel? 'Pro-forestation', allowing forests simply to grow on undisturbed to the end of their natural lives, is suggested as a better option than afforestation (new woods): the advantages are that no new land is required, no new costs are incurred, and the forest continues to sequester carbon at rates far above what was previously thought.

A mature beech avenue in West Dorset. But who planted the trees and why? Do they mark a long-forgotten ancient track into the nearby hamlet? Do they shelter crops or mark parish boundaries? Whoever planted them did not live to appreciate them fully grown. Yet without this tree-planter or group of planters, tree avenues, hedges and woods would not exist in our lives today.

Wood planting at Longdown, Devon. These trees are each individually protected from browsing by deer and rabbits. If we reduced excessive deer numbers, we would not need to use these plastic tubes, nor clear them up again ten years later. Photograph by Paul Harrison.

All that from just standing back and letting nature take over!

So when we're in the mood for planting trees, we should always pause for a moment and remind ourselves of what botanist and landscape historian Oliver Rackham once said: 'Planting is not conservation, but an admission that conservation has failed.'. Rackham believed that a planted tree is also a damaged tree, with poor root development and missing essential mycorrhizae – if people want to plant trees, they also need to look after them as they grow. However, Rackham's argument does accept that 'planting is all very well for replacing trees definitely known to have been planted, in plantations, gardens and arboreta.'

So how can we best help trees on their way? What can we do to start them on their long journey through the years? Should we be planting or making space for natural regeneration? As with most tree issues, we need both strategies. There is intense pressure on our land and it often requires decisive action to make the changes we want, such as greater tree cover. On the other hand, if mass tree planting is our latest attempt to shape the land, will we have learned anything of ourselves and of nature? Yet natural regeneration and planting are not mutually exclusive: they may be extremes in our attitude towards trees, but they are also methods that can be used side-by-side to establish new woods.

Tree planting has not been particularly important to other European Union countries because they have higher forest cover, so Common Agricultural Policy (CAP) funding favours agriculture over woods and forests. As the British Woodlands Survey of 2017 found, landowners who were willing to consider more tree planting were put off by the complexity of regulations, the lack of grant aid and the threats posed by deer and grey squirrels. This is why leaving the European Common Agricultural Policy must become an opportunity to reform rural subsidy payments, favouring instead a system that rewards a much wider range of social and environmental benefits, including greater support for trees and woods.

But even if the government establishes policies in favour of trees and woods, our future forest cover will still be shaped by the decisions of private farmers and landowners. Will they be persuaded to convert agricultural land to woodland? Can farmers find a way to combine more trees with agriculture? We need a more nuanced approach, giving nature as much free rein as possible and only intervening as much as is necessary. After all, we cannot actually make trees grow, we can only create the space in which they can work their magic.

Trees on the farm

Agricultural land is facing challenges of its own: arable land in Britain is losing soil and fertility at alarming rates. Heavier machinery, compaction, poor soil structure, waterlogging, lack of soil organic matter and quicker rotations have put soils under unprecedented stress. Not surprisingly, farmland biodiversity is also plummeting.

Trees can help with all of these issues, yet they are often seen as an extra burden on the farm, costing time or money: hedges

For many landowners, game birds are an essential economic mainstay of the woods: over 50 million are released each year. Organisations such as the British Game Alliance suggest that shooting them contributes £2 billion to the economy and supports 35,000 jobs. However, the release of such large numbers of non-native birds into the British countryside has been challenged by campaigners concerned about the impacts on native birds and habitats.

need to be machine-flailed every year, veteran trees need to be cleared away when they fall in a storm, and woods only find their value when used for rearing pheasants for game shooting. Yet trees and farms have co-existed more closely in the past, and could do again.

It hasn't helped that forestry and farming have evolved along separate pathways in recent decades, each developing their own professional practice, governance and, crucially, grant systems under the CAP. As a result, they are often sharply demarcated in the landscape and have come to be seen as competitors for land and investment. Farmers have had to choose between crops and trees. Often planting trees would result in loss of grant payments and a drop in land value, not to mention the commitment of that land to trees in perpetuity. Almost a third of farms are tenanted, and tenant farmers might not have the incentive (or permission) for long-term tree-planting initiatives.

Agricultural land is under great stress from our ever-greater demands for production, fostered by a perverse system of grants and hidden costs. Yet there is little opportunity for this land to approach anything like its natural state. So if we agree that trees are public goods providing social and environmental benefits, but they are not financially viable for farmers, surely they are

ideal candidates for targeted funding?

There is no shortage of ideas around at the moment about how Britain, no longer a member of the European Union, should reform agriculture and its funding. The Confederation of Forest Industries (Confor) believes that a 'Common Countryside Policy' should replace the EU Common Agricultural Policy and integrate farming and forestry once again. The Committee on Climate Change argues that cutting beef, lamb and dairy consumption by 20 per cent will free up farmland for trees, peatland and energy crops. The RSA (Royal Society for the encouragement of Arts, Manufactures and Commerce) sees farming as a force for change and advocates a transition to agroecological farming which works with natural systems, using techniques such as integrated pest management, organic farming, conservation and regenerative agriculture and agroforestry. The National Farmers Union are not so happy about this shift in land use, and

Pasture for livestock accounts for about half of farmland. This is about 35 per cent of the UK, so it represents an enormous area. Add to this the land used to grow feed for livestock, and animal agriculture occupies 48 per cent of all UK land. A modest change of diet away from animal products would free up a lot of land for trees, peatland and wild areas of all kinds. Photograph courtesy of David Levene.

Although wood-meadows are not an historical feature of the British landscape, wood-meadows such as this one in Laelatu, Estonia, demonstrate that as well as being biologically diverse they are also highly productive ways of growing both grass and leaves for animal fodder. Photograph by George Peterken.

although they do aim for net zero greenhouse gas emissions by 2040 the ambition for trees is very low, enhancing hedgerows and woodland planting accounting for just 2.6 per cent of the proposed CO_2 reductions. Meanwhile, the author Dieter Helm explores the 'crazy economics of British farming' from a Natural Capital perspective: if you count agriculture's £3 billion subsidy, its pollution costs, its inheritance-tax concessions and other exemptions, 'it is not implausible to suggest that the £9 billion gross output has an economic value that is close to zero'.

We now have an opportunity to redirect these government subsidies towards public payments for public goods, so the people who manage the land are rewarded for protecting, regenerating and sustaining it for us all. But it is not just land-use which we need to address. It's our diets, farming practice, landscape: nothing short of *all* our cultural attitudes to food and land. The array of ideas and solutions must also ask searching questions about what the land is for – or what it *should* be for – in Britain.

Wood and meadow are usually understood to be distinct habitats in the UK, but in reality they happily co-exist side-by-side in a mosaic of coppice and meadow, as seen at the Carmel Reserve in Carmarthenshire. Photograph by George Peterken.

Any implementation of new ideas will have to be thoughtfully planned, because each farmed landscape is different, and those who farm or own land will need advice and support to prepare for any shift of direction.

Fields with trees?

We need to explore new ways of integrating trees into the farmed landscape. Any new trees in the landscape must be carefully considered. We have to ask ourselves what trees are already there? What are the other valuable habitats? What food is this land producing? What species are most appropriate? Do we need to plant, or can we just step back and let it regenerate naturally? What sort of protection would the new trees need? What are the trees for? Much depends on the farmland itself, what it is and what it needs to help it become more resilient.

Arable farmland accounts for about one-third of agricultural

This apple and pear orchard in North Perrott, Somerset, is sheltered from the prevailing wind by fast-growing poplar trees, that are also harvested on rotation for woodfuel and timber.

land and production is important, especially as we only grow about half of our food. Planting trees extensively on high-grade land is a waste of a valuable resource, but we can actually improve arable land by the judicious planting of trees alongside the arable crops. Arable soils are especially vulnerable to drought and wind erosion, also to rain run-off and water erosion, but the strategic placement of shelterbelts, planted in strips or bands of trees, can help prevent both these problems. Any porous belt of trees can also create a microclimate that provides shelter up to 30 times its height, meaning less evapo-transpiration, lower wind speeds, less soil loss and less spray drift.

Moderating water flows is crucial to reducing the run-off of phosphates, nitrates and silt pollution into watercourses. Strips or bands of trees in an arable landscape can also provide shelter, habitat and food for pollinating insects and connecting highways of biodiversity. Existing hedges could be allowed to grow tall (if the right species are present), and could be periodically harvested for woodfuel or timber, as in the 'bocage' systems of northern France. Importantly, trees don't compete with shallow-rooted crops for light, nutrients and other resources because their crowns grow high and their roots (mostly) grow deep below. In fact, integrating trees much more into farmland will improve soil quality, biological diversity and resilience to

adverse weather and economic shocks.

Pasture for livestock accounts for about half of farmland. This is about 35 per cent of the UK, so it represents an enormous area. Whilst pasture does not face the same challenges as arable, it does have to provide a living environment for the animals grazing there: shade and shelter, browsing and fodder, and protected areas for the birth and care of their young. The more diverse the environment, the more likely animals can look after themselves and maintain a healthy balance.

Farmers in mid-Wales collaborated on the Pontbren Project to plant trees and hedges to improve conditions for their upland livestock. In doing so, they also reduced water run-off across the whole catchment and enhanced biodiversity. Crucial to their success was the strategic placement of the tree planting, the species used and their management.

Although farming and forestry, or agroforestry, has been much more integrated in Britain in the past, we must look to other parts of the world, especially the US and Europe, to see how we can combine trees with arable (silvo-arable) or with pasture (silvo-pastoral). In Britain there are examples of wood pasture (animals grazing amongst trees), such as the New Forest, woodland chickens and grazed orchards, but fewer arable examples.

In Suffolk, this is already happening with 'alley cropping' at

Let it grow! As Defra points out: 'With wire fences making many hedges obsolete as stock-proof barriers, less frequent cutting is once again appropriate for most hedges.' In Brittany, France, the periodic harvesting of hedges means that trees are allowed to integrate into farmland, creating an intimate and sheltered *bocage* landscape.

Eastbrook Farm, Wiltshire: organic dairy cows mob-grazing alongside strips of perry pears and willows planted for shelter and produce.

Wakelyns Farm, where rows of hazel, willow, fruit and timber trees are laid out with crops of cereals and vegetables (*see* case study opposite). In Wiltshire, trees have been integrated with organic cattle grazing at Eastbrook Farm, where Helen Browning is including parkland trees in pasture, browsing blocks of willow and poplar, and one big field has been planted mostly with strips of perry pears, willow and alder, with a few lines of timber trees such as oak, hornbeam and cherry. Each strip is 3 m wide and protected by an electric wire, with 24-metre strips of grazing between, so about 11 per cent of the land has been used. These strips suit her mob-grazing method, where the cattle graze one strip for a few days, then are moved on to the next. When the trees are big enough, the wire on one side may be removed to allow the cows to get in amongst the trees. The advantages of the trees are the additional crop of pears and the improved welfare for the cows, who have more shelter from the sun and the rain, alongside more diverse forage from the tree leaves.

As a strategy for increasing tree cover in the farmed landscape, arable agroforestry has much to commend it, with reports of

ALLEY CROPPING ON THE FARM

Set in the big fields of the mid-Suffolk plateau, there is a small island of radical farming. Instead of huge monocultural slabs of cereal, there is a rich mix of vegetables, legumes, cereals, clover leys, fruits and nuts, willow and hardwoods growing together – welcome to Wakelyns Agroforestry.

Wakelyns is a 23-hectare organic farm that has also been Ann and Martin Wolfe's research station since 1994, where they have pioneered both wheat populations and put agroforestry ideas into practice, growing an alternative production model to that of the surrounding Suffolk prairies. At the heart of their project is the intention to bring 'trees back into the centre of things'. Martin died in 2019, but his work and inspiration continue here and elsewhere.

On the farm, there are four silvo-arable systems on trial, all planted with 3-metre strips of trees running north–south (to minimise shading), dividing 12-metre or 18-metre alleys of crops that are wide enough for agricultural machinery.

There is hazel coppice producing high-grade thatching spars, hurdles, nuts and woodchip. The hazel is planted in double rows and one is cut every five years, keeping the protective hedge intact. The willow coppice works in a similar way, but the rapid growth is ready for cutting after just two years, producing a high volume of woodchip for the farm boiler and export to biomass suppliers.

There is also an area of orchard, with a wide variety of apples, pears, plums and other fruits growing as medium-sized trees in strips alongside the arable crops. Lastly, the timber trees are now some 9–12 metres high and include oak, ash, hornbeam, Italian alder, wild cherry, lime and sycamore.

Diversity is at the heart of Wakelyns. Ann and Martin observed that natural plant communities contain a wide variety of species and genes, which respond to environmental variation, such as weather, climate and diseases. This 'functional biodiversity' increases the resilience and productivity of the whole growing system, and also provides a wonderful place for humans to live and work.

Diversity is working in three dimensions, above

and below ground: there isn't just one wheat variety here, but a breeding population able to adapt; not a single produce but many, including fruits, nuts, coppice, firewood, timber, shelter, habitat, carbon sequestration – the benefits literally stack up.

Industrial intensification has led to simplified landscapes with standardised crops for maximum production. Wakelyns has developed a benign complexity more akin to the abundance of nature. It is a beautiful little landscape, both intimate and busy, familiar but radical. If ever we needed agricultural production which is resilient, biodiverse, free from energy-intensive inputs and toxic outputs, protective and human-scale, the time is now!

After walking up and down the cropping alleys, sampling the ripe fruits, imagining a future farming with trees, it is a shock stepping out into the big, bland surrounding fields, a sudden exposure, and a reminder of the challenges ahead.

WAKELYNS: wakelyns.co.uk
AGROFORESTRY RESEARCH TRUST: agroforestry.co.uk

total yields (for crops and trees) from 10 to 40 per cent higher than arable alone. Yet this innovative land-use is hampered by the fact that the current grant systems treat the agriculture and forestry components separately, making integrated management difficult. At Eastbrook, subsidy payments to the farm have decreased because of a perceived loss of area to trees, although the actual grazing area has barely reduced. This could – and must – change with more enlightened policies that accept trees as part of the farmed landscape.

Into the radical uplands

The most radical way to increase tree cover would be to convert much of our marginal agricultural uplands to forest. Trees have a huge role to play in towns, gardens and farmland, but if we are serious about substantially increasing forest cover this may be the most suitable land for large-scale gains in tree cover.

Confor points out that in the case of farming livestock on the uplands of Scotland and Wales, farms tend to lose money before subsidies, yet forestry trades at a surplus. In Wales, the upfront costs of planting can be met by government grants with any investment repaid ten-fold with public benefits to the Welsh economy, air quality, carbon storage and recreation.

Friends of the Earth has addressed the task of 'finding the land to double tree cover' in England and come up with a plausible suggestion: 'If we continue to shift our diets to eating less and better meat and dairy, we'll be able to free up a lot of land that's currently used for pasture, especially low-grade rough pasture and cropland that's used for livestock feed.' They would avoid planting on high-quality agricultural land and peat bogs, and instead focus planting on the 1.6 million hectares of rough grazing, which would more than double England's forest cover. About a quarter of this is near urban areas and could be 'easily accessible to millions of people'.

So why don't hill farms convert to forestry if it is so much more profitable? For a start, the farming subsidies turn losses into modest profits. And not everyone is driven by profits – they say hill farmers are born not made, and 'giving up' land to forestry can seem like a failure. Indeed, there has been a

Room for more trees? Welsh uplands (*above*) with forestry and rough grazing, while near Bridport in Dorset grazed downlands (*left*) are re-clothing themselves in scrub and naturally regenerating trees, although there is room for more thickets and open-grown, individual trees – if allowed to grow!

backlash by some farmers against people making alternative plans for their land: this is people's livelihoods, history and culture at stake. Farmers know about farming and may not have the interest in or skills for designing, planting and managing upland plantations. Handing over control of their land to a forest management company may also be unappealing.

For investors there is uncertainty about permission and grants for large-scale planting projects, so they are reluctant to buy land which may turn out not to be plantable. Also, suitable land only rarely comes up for sale. It may be that once some pioneering farmers work with the forestry industry, their example will change cultural attitudes.

The UK's Committee on Climate Change issued reports in 2018 and 2020 calling for fundamental reform of our unsustainable land use. They observe that policy has long favoured food production over other land uses and that 'it has not rewarded other services, including adaptation to climate change and carbon sequestration and storage'. In the report, they advocate low-carbon farming practices, deep emissions reductions, restoration of peatlands, reduced meat consumption and a doubling or trebling of careful tree planting. This is asking for us to fundamentally reconsider what our land is *for*.

Is land for growing food? Is land for growing profits? It may turn out that other claims on it are much more urgent: carbon sequestration, water regulation, wildlife habitat, and even our food-producing land needs greater protection from the elements. Landowners may find themselves in a similar position to factory-owners at the outbreak of war: their assets – our public goods – might be urgently needed to meet an existential crisis.

Farmers face continual risk – from unpredictable weather, drought, floods, disease, price fluctuations, market access, most recently from uncertainty over vital subsidies – and these risks will become worse with climate breakdown. We already depend on farmers to provide food and look after the land and now we are asking them to address climate concerns too. We need to find a way of supporting farmers and land managers to do the right thing, whilst supporting the public to make the right choices.

An even more radical approach by Dr Helen Harwatt, a food

Tree shelters, stakes and cell-grown trees on a White Rose Forest planting site in West Yorkshire, which is part of a planting project to cover the Leeds City Region and join with other efforts to establish England's Northern Forest.

and climate specialist, suggests 'repurposing UK agricultural land to meet climate goals'. One scenario maximises carbon dioxide removal 'by restoring land currently under pasture and cropland used to produce farmed animal feed to forest' – that means no more farm animals. Dr Harwatt estimates that 48 per cent of land in the UK is used for animal agriculture, so if we stopped all that and diverted it to trees, it would take our forest cover to over 60 per cent.

Such an approach has long been advocated by The Movement for Compassionate Living, to address the combined challenges of world population growth, climate change, animal welfare and environmental degradation. This is a vision for a tree-based culture with no farm animals, where orchards of tree crops provide most of our protein and carbohydrates.

Although it is unlikely for the foreseeable future, if ever, that the UK will be meat- and dairy-free it is important to question the limitations of our current attitude to land, and ponder how trees might fulfil a much greater proportion of our needs.

Climate breakdown is a reality and the shocks and pressures it is already creating demand that we reconsider the fundamental ways in which our land is used. Living more closely with trees will make us more resilient in the future.

If we do decide that we want more trees in our lives, if we want to double (or more) tree cover, most of these will have to be planted or regenerated naturally on farmland of some sort. Planting grazing land with trees may be a desirable way to reduce carbon emissions, but not if we then import just as much beef from ranches raising cattle on deforested parts of the Amazon.

We need to find a new balance between the food we grow and eat, the materials we use, and our wider ecological support network. What might that landscape look like? How would it feel to inhabit? How could it come into being?

Planting new forests

There are many targets out there for tree planting – national targets, corporate targets, campaign targets, political targets – so what should we aim for? Targets reveal our ambition (or lack thereof) and are helpful to focus our intentions and resources. But what do the targets actually mean?

Let's start with our state forestry services in England, Scotland, Wales and Northern Ireland, which aim to increase UK tree cover from the current 13 per cent to around 17 per cent by planting at a rate of 22,000–27,000 hectares per year. Compared to historic rates, these targets are close to the 'investment' era of the 1970s and 1980s, yet the reality on the ground is very different. In fact, the rate of tree planting has been declining steadily since 2000 and has reached an all-time low in the last decade of about 5,500 hectares per year. Meanwhile, there are signs that England is currently losing more woodland to development and infrastructure than is being planted.

The Woodland Trust would like to increase UK woodland cover to 19 per cent by 2050 'to tackle this country's biodiversity and climate crises'. This would mean an additional 1.5 million hectares

THE URBAN WOOD

Horsenden Hill, a 300-acre mix of Ancient Semi-Natural Woodland and grassland, is the largest single nature conservation site in Ealing, West London. The falling demand for timber cropping and hay to support horse-drawn transport during the 1800s meant that much of the ancient oakwood was clearfelled and what little remained became unmanaged and returned to scrub. Although it supported some natural regeneration, Horsenden Hill lacked biodiversity, high-canopy woodland and had a low proportion of veteran trees.

Since 2017, Ealing Council, Trees for Cities and the local community have been collaborating to restore and revive an urban woodland for the twenty-first century. Reconnecting Horsenden Hill with its community inspired the planting of 'Whittlers', a new wood growing a wide variety of tree species for resilience to climate change

and improved biodiversity. Native hardwoods and softwoods (beech, oak, lime and Scots pine) provide a long-term timber crop whilst hazel and birch provide a coppice harvest every 5 to 7 years on rotation. Over 800 community volunteers were involved in planting over 9,500 trees.

A small number of 150-year-old plantation oaks were also harvested – local makers used the timber to craft benches, gates and fencing for Horsenden Hill. Furniture-making and woodcraft courses are now run from the site as part of a new social enterprise approach to improve access for nearby Belvue School and the elderly and vulnerable clients of local charity, Neighbourly Care. A community orchard has also been planted, with fruit and nut trees for all to enjoy.

Engaging the community in planning and planting new forests could ensure they value and care for them in the longer term. Today, The Friends of Horsenden Hill help maintain the site and raise funds to support its ongoing management.

NEW UPLAND FOREST

We are desperately short of trees, woods and forests in England, yet there can be a strange official presumption against planting more trees.

We have grown accustomed to extensive open habitats in the uplands, despite the fact that they are ecological anomalies in our temperate climate, and disturbing this status quo can be challenging.

Enter Andy Howard. One of his clients wanted to invest long-term in upland forestry and bought the land at Doddington North Moor. They embarked on getting planting approval for the largest productive plantation in England for decades. In Scotland this can take just eight to ten months. In Northumberland it took over two years, and turned into a crusade to get the right trees planted in the right place.

Much of the proposed 354-hectare scheme was designated as 'upland heathland', a Priority Habitat that should not be planted over. But Andy challenged this blanket designation, showing that the land was a more interesting mosaic of habitats.

Then Natural England's ecological survey revealed lowland raised mire, lowland wet and dry heath, lowland acid grassland and wet woodland – which formed the basis of a set of 'traffic light' principles to inform conservation and planting. As a result, the genuinely high-priority 'red' habitats are being restored (eg removal of rhododendron and trees from the mires); the intermediate 'amber' zones are still priority habitat and are being maintained, including low-density planting of native trees; the remaining 'green' zones are of very low conservation interest and can be planted with productive conifers.

There is still room for the commercially productive core of the project – some 42 per cent of the scheme is Sitka spruce – but this is far lower than some upland plantations. The Sitka is down on the lower land, away from the priority habitats and off the skyline (a concern of the nearby Northumberland National Park).

Local people have long memories and don't want 'another Kielder' – more monocultural blots on the landscape. Andy has taken the trouble at local meetings and events to explain how modern forestry has to be much more closely suited to the land and to local people these days.

Forestry Commission grants have been crucial to the project: the Woodland Creation Planning Grant reduced the risk and cost of the long planning process; the owner's investment was also supplemented by the innovative Woodland Carbon Fund, the Woodland Carbon Code and inheritance tax allowance.

This project has challenged assumptions about landscape, conservation and forestry, and found a creative solution where everyone has gained something – the owner has a viable investment; a productive forest will yield the wood we need; priority habitats are improved; planting targets get a boost; the local public enjoy access to a more diverse landscape; Andy realises his vision for modern upland forestry.

DODDINGTON NORTH AFFORESTATION PROJECT: doddingtonnorthforest.com

of woodland, mostly native trees, to address both nature and climate crises together. They also point out that 'the UK faces the loss of approximately 150 million mature trees . . . to ash dieback disease in the next 10 to 20 years'.

The Committee on Climate Change agrees that we must at least *triple* current planting rates to about 30,000 hectares per year until 2050, covering over 1 million hectares and increasing forest cover from 13 per cent to 17 per cent. It also offers a 'further ambition' scenario where 50,000 hectares are planted per year, raising cover to 19 per cent. At about 1,500 trees per hectare, that's 1.5 billion trees!

However, the Centre for Alternative Technology and Friends of the Earth think we should double the ambitions of the Woodland Trust and Committee on Climate Change, with an additional 3 million hectares of forest (doubling the forest area in the UK): as the UK 'powers down' our energy demands and 'powers up' our use of renewable energy, carbon capture will become a significant part of becoming a zero carbon nation.

Worldwide, there are similar targets and calls for massive restoration of the world's forests to deal with the twin threats of biodiversity loss and carbon pollution. The WWF, for example, has launched the 'Trillion Trees' programme of re-growing trees, saving them from loss and protecting them better.

The planned Northern Forest from Hull to Liverpool was announced in 2018, with support from the Woodland Trust and the Community Forest Trust. This new forest aims to plant 50 million trees over 25 years at an overall cost of £500 million. The social, economic and environmental benefits are estimated to be five times the investment, at around £2.5 billion. Yet the government has committed only £5.7 million to the project, just 1 per cent of what it needs.

Finally, there is political consensus for more trees in the UK, but increasing planting by an order of magnitude will require increases in funding and a streamlining of the application processes for large schemes. Politicians love to announce that they are planting millions of trees, but do they talk about how to plant all these trees and care for them once they're in the ground? It is much more useful to know how many hectares will be planted, what species and where.

A productive conifer plantation, for example, with close rows to promote straight growth, would have about 2,250–2,500 trees per hectare (spaced at about 2 m x 2 m). Productive broadleaves such as oak and beech, sycamore, sweet chestnut or hazel, might be 1,600 trees per hectare, whereas a wood planted for biodiversity might be around 1,100 trees per hectare (spaced at 3 m x 3 m). So the promise of 1 million trees could cover anywhere from 400 to 900 hectares, and an annual target of planting 30,000 hectares actually means about 60 million trees.

As we can see, targets are useful but they do also reduce the issues to a level of abstraction. They might offer us a snapshot or one way of looking at the issues from the here and now, but it is not a case of adding a few per cent here or doubling numbers there. Rather, it is about working out what sort of tree cover the UK requires for the challenges ahead, then steering all efforts and resources to achieving it. Not 'how much land can we afford to put down to trees?' Instead, we need to ask: *What tree cover do we need for a viable island? What is the least we need for a sustainable and ecologically functioning landscape?*

The benefits of planting millions of trees and creating our viable island can easily be wiped out by continuing to subsidise fossil fuel use at home and abroad. It is easy to sound like you are acting on the climate emergency by announcing a massive tree planting campaign, but continuing business as usual elsewhere. Reducing CO_2 emissions is absolutely vital and will require tough choices and robust programmes across all government departments and councils. Tree planting is not a substitute for this, but can absorb carbon from the atmosphere and help mitigate the flooding of towns and villages in valleys that are surrounded by uplands and moorlands.

We also need to spend much more time asking what sorts of trees need to be planted and where. And in places where trees are already growing, we also need to ask whether natural regeneration is a better option. The ecologist Keith Kirby warns that concentrating on 30 per cent forest cover, with the rest of the land in intensive arable, would almost certainly be worse for biodiversity, and suggests that we should aim for 15 per cent woodland in a wider 'matrix of unimproved meadows, scattered trees and hedges'. George Peterken, another eminent ecologist

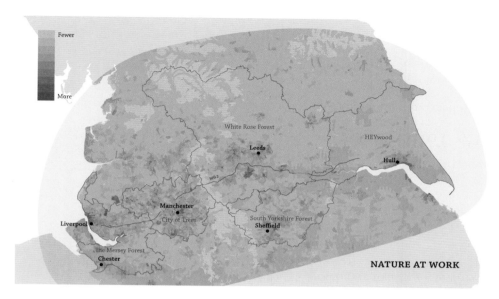

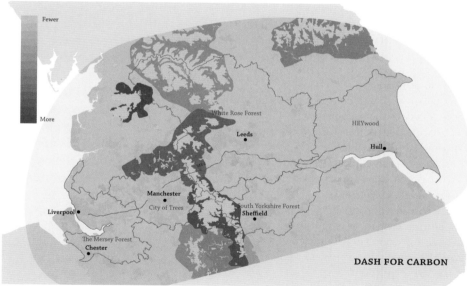

We must urgently address carbon emissions, and part of the UK's plans should be to cover much more land with trees for this reason alone. Our heavily deforested countryside means we have abundant land that is marginal for agriculture and would be suitable for trees. The Woodland Trust have modelled two approaches for the Northern Forest, delivering quite different outcomes. The 'Dash for Carbon' favours fast-growing conifer plantations in the Pennines for rapid carbon sequestration; whilst 'Nature@Work' shows the same area of tree cover, but composed of native woodland, commercial plantations and trees outside woods, yielding greater benefits for carbon, flood management, health and wellbeing and ecological restoration. Image courtesy of the Woodland Trust.

and writer, argues for extensive forest cover to minimise ecological isolation, linking these together with well-wooded corridors focused on riparian zones and floodplains. Peterken also recommends managing existing woods to provide a full range of habitats and open spaces to make the landscape as permeable as possible to woodland and open-ground species.

Ideally, every parish and town should be encouraged to develop a vision for trees and woods in their locality, starting with a tree map of the area that can draw out what the needs, threats, tree species and human relationships are in that particular landscape.

Rewilding

The ideas and projects in this book seek to redress the fundamental imbalance in our relationship with nature: more trees in towns, a more diverse farmed landscape, spending more time in the woods. Rewilding initiatives go even further by placing nature and natural processes at the very centre of the project, restoring some of the wild matrix within which we used to live, and could live again.

This is not turning back the clock to re-create some version of a lost landscape; it is restoring the wild processes under which those landscapes operated. It aims to encourage the ebb and flow of grazing and scrub growth (as championed by the ecologist Hans Vera and his vision of wildwood), or the natural regeneration of trees, 'weeds' and their associated fauna. The landscape is not a fixed structure that we seek to conserve or restore, but an ongoing and infinite ecological process of flow and change, growth and decay, which we can *choose* to enable.

In the words of Alan Watson Featherstone, visionary ecologist and founder of Trees for Life in Scotland, rewilding is 'the whole process of returning ecosystems to a state of ecological health and dynamic balance, making them self-sustaining, without the need for ongoing human management.'

Rewilding a landscape begins with the vegetation, the base of the food chain. In upland landscapes, for example, this usually means restoring the protective mantle of tree and shrub cover, at least in part. With so few parent trees to supply seed, this

Creag Meagaidh National Nature Reserve (*above*) covers 4,000 hectares in the south of the Monadhliath, north of Loch Laggan in Scotland. This was one of the first places in Scotland to take a serious approach to reversing centuries of land degradation. The aim was to enable the natural regeneration of woodland and forest by reducing the number of deer without planting new trees.

Ghosts of wildwood in Lairig Ghru (*left*), a central glen of the massif in the Cairngorms. These bleached stumps of pine have been exposed in eroded peat hags. They would have been sizeable trees in their time, possibly some 800 years ago. Once the trees died, the slow creep of peat, deepening by a millimetre a year, would have overtaken the valley. Imagine a wood here in this deep glen, where today there is not a tree in sight.

often requires planting of native species. And if trees are already growing, they need protecting from browsing sheep and deer so that natural regeneration can take place. As trees and shrubs return, so do the flowers and grasses and fungi. When the plants have established, insects can return to feed and breed on them and contribute to the cycling of nutrients.

After the vegetation and invertebrates have established, the vertebrates follow on as the next trophic layer: birds, mammals and other creatures feed on the insects and spread seed in their droppings. A functioning ecology begins to develop. And people are part of the rewilding. This is not a project to create a wildlife park without humans, but an opportunity to relax our control on the land. Instead of us forcing nature to do our bidding, we allow nature to lead the way for us all.

The journalist and author George Monbiot has called for rewilding to be started on 10 per cent of our uplands, but because our landscapes have been so thoroughly altered over thousands of years, it isn't always clear what returning them to 'the wild' means. It presents a peculiar challenge: these landscapes might be bare and devoid of suitable species, or they may be full to bursting with inappropriate species.

Paradoxically, rewilding often requires some preparatory work – controlling some undesirable species (eg excessive deer, rhododendron, grey squirrels) and also adding missing species that would not otherwise appear (eg wood ants, beavers). We are still intervening, and as the trophic layers build up, higher predators could also be supported. They may arrive naturally, but often need to be introduced from far away, which creates further, intriguing dilemmas about how wild we want to be.

When we stop suppressing the 'self-willed' inclination of the land to clothe itself in vegetation, we allow the land to express itself according to its nature. We allow wildlife to return and recolonise. We restore one small mosaic tile to the whole, contributing to a new pattern in the landscape and new meanings in our lives. Key ecological functions are also restored: improved carbon storage, flood mitigation, hydrological cycles with better water quality, nutrient cycles building up fertility. The result is a more diverse and resilient forest and landscape.

The charity Rewilding Britain recently proposed a new vision

HIGHLAND REWILDING

During the last Ice Age, the mountains of the Cairngorms were covered in ice sheets and glaciers hundreds of metres thick, grinding down peaks and gouging out glens. As the climate warmed, plants and animals crept across the tundra and up the valleys, building soil and habitat, forming scrub of willow and juniper and woods of birch, Scots pine, hazel and aspen. A rich mosaic spread out across the Highlands, with dense stands of forest, clumps of trees and scrub, open grassland, heathland and bog, and probably reached its greatest extent in about 3000 BC. This was 'peak wildwood' in Scotland.

More than half of this wildwood was gone before the Romans arrived down south, and even more was razed by fire and grazing in the following centuries, reaching a particular low in the eighteenth century. At Mar Lodge Estate, the remains of wildwood were under pressure from crofters seeking firewood and building materials in the 1700s, and from the estate owners expanding logging and cattle grazing. Then sheep farming brought more hungry browsers to the glens, soon to be replaced in the nineteenth century by the new fashion for deer stalking and the eradication of any animals considered a threat to the 'sport'. In one ten-year period, the five parishes from Mar Lodge to Ballater record killing 634 foxes, 44 wildcats, 57 polecats, 70 eagles, 2520 hawks and kites, 1347 ravens and hooded crows, not to mention those 'destroyed by poison, or died of their wounds'.

Now only about 1 per cent of the original wildwood and its inhabitants remains in Scotland, and this is still being razed by huge numbers of deer. But we could be at a turning point as post-glacial vegetation begins its slow return across the (almost) bare land for a second time. Over recent decades, in the cleared hillsides and scoured glens of the Highlands, large-scale restoration projects have emerged, protecting remnant clumps of Caledonian pine, regenerating them and adding more native woodland to the landscape.

The Cairngorms are blessed with three such projects: Abernethy in the north (RSPB), Mar Lodge in the south (National Trust for Scotland) and Glenfeshie in the west (private estate). Though the high plateau would not be suitable for trees, the National Park has mapped the intervening glens as suitable for woods, or at least scattered trees and shrubs: eventually they could stretch out along the glens to link up.

The remaining trees are stands of 'granny pines' up to 200 years old, which used to be stranded alone in seas of heather. But Mar Lodge is on its way to doubling its area of Caledonian pinewood. Much of this restoration is 'rewilding', in the sense that the trees, plants and animals are colonising new ground themselves. People are still intervening, but instead of contributing to the destruction, they are trying to establish a more authentic ecological balance where natural flora and fauna can thrive. Sometimes, the parent populations are no longer present, so planting and re-introduction of species is necessary to fill the gaps.

There are few sights more heartening than to see a scattering of young pines now growing up around gnarled veteran trees, made possible at Mar Lodge by a drastic reduction in deer. Here, in these hard-worn hills, the over-exploitation of the land has been reined in and nature allowed to reclaim and re-clothe the land.

REWILDING BRITAIN: rewildingbritain.org.uk

combining landscape restoration and carbon sequestration. By redirecting agricultural subsidies towards the public good of capturing carbon, they envisage substantial payments to farmers for new woodland, peat bogs, wildflower meadows and ponds, with annual payments reflecting the carbon absorbed. This could be rolled out over one quarter of the UK, including 'allowing natural forest regeneration on 2 million hectares of land currently used for low-species-diversity grassland'.

The wide open mountains of Scotland are home to many rewilding projects, including Trees for Life (in Glenn Moriston and Glen Affric), Carrifran Woodland (a community project in the Borders) and several in the Cairngorms: Glenfeshie Estate, Abernethy (RSPB) and Mar Lodge Estate (National Trust for Scotland). At Mar Lodge, the late-eighteenth-century Clearances and subsequent sheep farming reduced the tree cover in the valleys above Braemar. Deer stalking became popular in the nineteenth century, boosted by Queen Victoria's visits, and the high deer numbers have prevented tree regeneration ever since, as they have elsewhere in the Cairngorms, leaving isolated ancient pine trees hanging on in a vast prairie of heather. Here, in order to restore the natural dynamics and ecology of the landscape, red deer numbers have been drastically reduced – and sure enough, the trees are returning. Already, a new generation of pine, birch and rowan are popping up out of the heather, reclaiming their rightful place in the land; it shows the extraordinary ability of wild nature to heal its wounds.

In Wild Ennerdale, a valley at the edge of the Lake District National Park in Cumbria, they have a slightly different problem: there are too many trees of the wrong sort. The valley was planted extensively (and controversially) with Sitka spruce in the middle of the twentieth century, and this had two curious effects: whilst it created a forbidding block of impenetrable plantation, it also 'protected the soils, the meandering river, some of the valley bottom wetlands and a rich archaeology from negative impacts of post-war agricultural intensification.'

The introduction of the exotic spruce also ironically provided a food source for the return of the native red squirrels. Now the main landowners are collaborating to develop a more natural and wild landscape: to replace this regimented industrial conifer crop

A rowan tree (*above*) planted at Bwlch Corog near Cwmyrhaiadr, Mid Wales. The site was acquired from the Woodland Trust for Cambrian Wildwood, a community initiative to restore native habitats and bring back lost native animals. The site is 140 hectares of moorland dominated by purple moor grass (*Molinia caerulea*), with a relatively small area of ancient woodland. The aim for Bwlch Corog is for native woodland to colonise naturally. However, in order to support this long process and provide a seed source in a treeless upland landscape, 8,000 native trees are being planted (*below*) in small groups across the site.

At Knepp Estate, Sussex, an observation platform overlooks former farmland that has been naturally regenerated with scrub and trees. Tree cover has increased from 10 to 42 per cent over 15 years.

with a mixture of broadleaf woodland, glades for grazing animals, scrub and thicket, with some retained conifers lower down the valley. Central to the plan is the River Liza, which will be allowed to meander and braid, creating new habitats as it flows.

Most interesting is the role of grazing cattle here. After the dense conifer was felled, the bare land was left – some was grazed and some was fenced off. The fenced area developed trees, shrubs and heather, whilst the grazed area was kept as rough grass. However, as the trees grew behind the fence, the canopy closed and species diversity started declining. Meanwhile, the cattle in the grazed area started wandering further afield, reducing the grazing pressure, which led to increased diversity of habitat and species, with meadow, scrub and trees. The cattle also disturbed the dense turf on higher ground to enable tree colonisation there.

Wild Ennerdale has developed a 'hybrid vision' to suit its situation, aiming for a 'future natural' landscape – that is to say, not a replica of some past ecosystem, but a valley where both native and exotic species can develop using both natural processes and some intervention – a valley 'thriving not just surviving'.

Not all habitats benefit from such an approach. The Wildlife Trusts point out that human intervention has shaped our land for 7,000 years, creating open habitats with special features that require our intervention to survive – habitats such as coppice

woodland, wildflower meadows, wood pasture, wood meadows and heathland. This highlights the importance of balance in the landscape – some land will be intensively farmed, some could benefit from rewilding, some jewels of conservation will continue to be managed as now.

Rewilding presents a challenge to us. Trees for Life believes it 'runs directly counter to human attempts to control nature'. Isabella Tree, in her account of the rewilding of Knepp Farm in Sussex, describes the process as 'giving nature the space and opportunity to express itself'. There is no set destination for the land at places such as Knepp and Wild Ennerdale: they have assembled the constituent parts (particularly grazing animals) and stepped back to watch the natural processes unfold with minimal intervention.

Wild Ennerdale: This valley has been transformed from conifer monoculture to a diverse mix of forest, scrub and grassland. Here we see natural regeneration of Rowan amongst heather. Photograph courtesy of Wild Ennerdale.

Abernethy National Nature Reserve, Cairngorms National Park, Scotland. The RSPB has reduced red deer numbers to allow the native Caledonian Pinewoods to return, along with their flora and fauna.

We have lived out of balance with nature for so long that the rewilding agenda can appear shocking to some – can we really abandon our hard-won countryside to beavers and wolves? These wild mammals are great for making headlines but aren't the whole story, and simply reflect that the main obstacle to new and radical landscape ideas is public opinion. There are many examples worldwide of successful re-introductions of sea eagles, ospreys, beavers, pine martens and wolves; and a growing number of rewilding projects in Britain, showing what is possible in just a few years once we let nature loose again. So the constraints are not technical but social, even personal. This very challenge can be an opportunity to engage the local community, to discuss their currently depleted surroundings, address concerns and to show the benefits of a richer ecosystem.

Of course, another objection to rewilding is utilitarian: can we afford to let the land just do what it likes? Where every acre has been pressed for profit over centuries, what of the rural economy and the countryside if we just give up? We need to retain productive agricultural land for food, but we know that many upland farms are only sustained through public subsidy and even lowland farmed estates can struggle to make a profit – part of the reason Knepp changed its course. Rewilding offers alternative income streams from visitors, hikers, ecotourism and modest harvests from woodfuel and grazing stock. And from a biodiversity point of view, can we afford *not* to have a hinterland of wild nature to support our islands of civilisation? So perhaps a compromise in some places might be to promote rewilding projects for 25 years, to restore the soil and ecological processes, such as fallow fields, then clear it again for agriculture if required. This could replace the CAP policy of field 'set aside' with longer-term rotations, where areas of a farm could undergo a regeneration programme.

Rewilding is clearly a very different approach to our current methods of control and intervention. Yet instead of pitting one against the other, we can see them as opposite ends of a spectrum: control at one end, leaving things to nature at the other. Indeed, it is already common in forestry practice and woodland management (*see* page 176) to mix intervention and rewilding: planting trees over part of an area and leaving some to natural regeneration from surrounding seed sources. There is certainly a place for both intervention and rewilding in the way we think about trees and woods, so perhaps it isn't such a radical shift to let more of the land run wild too.

Repairing the web of life

How can we repair the threadbare web of life? And how can we include ourselves in it? Can we make decisions *with* nature rather than *dominating* nature? What role might trees play in repairing the ecological landscape?

As we have seen, George Peterken's vision of linking and planting within existing woodland and farmland habitats could establish a permeable 'Forest Habitat Network' for all wildlife. The afforestation of the last century has contributed something towards this, but because it has been so haphazard, not part of a landscape-wide vision, it has resulted in isolated woods on remote hillsides or small woods surrounded by hostile agricultural landscapes. Peterken argues for 'Core Forest Areas, large forests and dense clusters of woods which harbour large and diverse populations of woodland species.' These areas would need to be at least 30 per cent wooded before 'the landscape

Moor Tree volunteers planting at Brook Manor, Buckfastleigh, Devon. Community hedge planting like this, with occasional standard trees, will make a real contribution of new habitats to the landscape.

starts to function as if it were a single, large wood for most woodland species.'

In 2010, similar ideas were proposed for England in *Making Space for Nature*, an independent review that looked at whether wildlife sites are capable of responding and adapting to the growing challenges of climate breakdown: 'The essence of what needs to be done to enhance the resilience and coherence of England's ecological network can be summarised in four words: more, bigger, better and joined.' The author of that report, Professor John Lawton, an ecologist and chair of the Royal Commission on Environmental Pollution, estimated the cost of establishing a coherent and resilient network to be in the range of £600 million to £1.1 billion per year. This is an interesting price tag. Compare this to the cost of bank bail-outs in 2007–10 (£133 billion), the projected annual pre-COVID costs of the NHS (£162 billion in 2020), the annual spending on debt interest (£52 billion) or total public spending (£848 billion in 2020). Just imagine the social, environmental and economic benefits this tiny portion of public spending would bring. Although the Lawton report focused only on England, its lessons can be applied throughout the UK.

The government's own Natural Environment White Paper

The Natural Choice (2011) adopted Professor Lawton's idea of ecological restoration zones and rebranded them Nature Improvement Areas (NIAs), but offered just £7.5 million of funding over three years, which is again only about 1 per cent of what Lawton suggested was necessary. The government's lack of progress towards its own goals is stark: the Natural Capital Committee, an independent advisor to the government, also called for the 25 Year Environment Plan to be underpinned in law because: 'Business as usual is going to lead to failure'.

The Wildlife Trusts have a similar approach to Lawton with their Living Landscapes initiative. Rather than focus on individual nature reserves, the focus is on landscape-scale conservation, 'whole river catchments and entire tracts of upland'. Like George Peterken, the Trusts work with core areas where sites of special importance can be linked by corridors of suitable habitat: these are stepping stones, which can make the whole landscape more permeable to wildlife. The Wildlife Trusts believe 'it is possible to achieve A Living Landscape across the

First the road crossed the land, then a land-bridge was built to cross the road. When fragmented habitats are re-connected, wildlife can range more freely and the risk of collisions is reduced. Photograph by Sergey Dzyuba.

Treesponsibility seeks to address climate change, improve biodiversity and engage community action by working through the medium of trees. In particular, it has collaborated on projects to stop the flooding in Hebden Bridge, by creating a much more wooded landscape and slowing the flow of water off the surrounding bare moorland.

UK in 30 years – a single generation – but only if opportunities are seized now.' With 4.5 million people in the UK members of Wildlife Trusts, the Woodland Trust or other conservation organisations, compared to only about 1 million members of political parties, it is time we make our collective will known.

From conquest to belonging?

Humans have come a long way since hunter-gathering in the wildwood. After all the transformations in human history – towards settled agricultural communities, towards science and industry, towards the data and information age – forests, woods and trees have been amongst the many casualties along our path to 'progress'. They have been cut down, poisoned, suppressed, controlled, domesticated and ignored. As we face physical and cultural crises across the globe, we have the opportunity to shape values that restore the web of life and rediscover where we belong inside it. By transforming our societies and landscapes *with* trees, by stitching trees into the fabric of our daily lives, we will also be responding to the damage our species has done to

Extinction Rebellion protest in London, October 2019. Our leaders have failed us, leaving children to make the case for urgent change.

the living world around us. As the theologian and poet Rowan Williams puts it, we need 'a fresh sense of the importance of living in attunement with who we are and what the world is.'

So instead of always asking what trees give us, perhaps it is time to ask ourselves: *what can we give trees*?

After the devastations of the Second World War, when we faced overwhelming public need, a bold vision was implemented to care for everyone: the National Health Service was born some 70 years ago, funded by everyone, open to everyone. We still invest in the health of the nation and public education because we see them as national priorities, as public goods. The current state of nature in Britain (and in the wider world) is in similarly desperate need of support and investment. We need a healthy natural world just as much as we need healthy bodies and resilient communities. And such support is unlikely to materialise from the free market.

In 2018–19 the UK government spent about £5.7 billion per year on agriculture, fisheries and forestry, £1.5 billion on environmental protection, £0.5 billion on protection of biodiversity. That's a total of about £7.7 billion from an annual public spending budget of £821 billion. That's less than 1 per cent. Why is our natural home such a low priority? Why do we take it for granted?

Trees already provide a natural health service and, as we have seen, they provide a web of life support to everyone. So we say it is time for a 'National Nature Service' – an NHS for Nature – with trees providing the framework. It should be publicly funded, serving us all; an annual allocation of public spending for nature, so that strategic tree planting and regeneration can be financed, alongside support for landowners, farmers, community groups, parish councils, town councils, county councils, schools, hospitals, charities and social enterprises, to care for trees and manage their woods for the common good. Farmers would benefit from greater emphasis on ecological farming practices and greater integration of trees in the landscape. Species in decline would benefit from joined-up conservation strategies to make the UK landscape more habitable and permeable. Instead of funding just 1 per cent of restoration initiatives, the government would be able to lead the way, and private investment would surely follow as opportunities for new enterprises emerged.

There are always competing demands on public spending, but it must surely be the most urgent need to safeguard our living planet, the very basis of everything else. A National Nature Service would establish a new era of care for nature, and ourselves within nature. A service *for* nature, rather than demanding services *from* nature. In the twentieth century, a bold idea emerged: a nation, through the NHS, can care collectively for the health of each other. The twenty-first century needs another bold idea, one that extends our circle of care beyond ourselves, to sustain the health of the natural world so that it can continue to sustain us.

As this book is going to print, the coronavirus pandemic is disrupting our globalised civilisation. We do not yet know how this will end, but three things are already clear: this disease has spread to humans from our unhealthy exploitation of nature, in particular of wild animals; in response to a global emergency, governments can react with staggering and effective measures previously unimaginable; as business as usual is paused, we can

see that wild nature is all around us, patiently waiting to resume when given the chance. We must remember all these lessons as we seek to knit our world back together.

A common feature of the projects described throughout this book is that they all originate in a particular place, borne of particular needs and opportunities, powered by particular people. These shoots of local action are pushing up through the cracks of our faltering society – the wild expressing itself. We need to celebrate these pioneers and dreamers. But at the same time, we need to acknowledge our limitations. Whenever we impose our will on nature, we cannot be sure what the response will be – often it has led to disaster on a global scale. It's all very well 'making plans for nature', but we must also be ready to stand back, watch and listen. Nature is not chaotic, yet neither is it as predictable as we might like. Nature is complex, nuanced, rebellious, surprising, resilient, always pursuing its own dynamics.

Nature and people can only be pushed so far. Now we need to stand up for ourselves and for the integrity of nature. Living with more trees in our lives can show us a deeper connection with nature, and help us to accept our place in the web of life.

Primal gathering: part of us has never left the forest. We connect deeply with the natural world and with each other in the woods. Can we restore these threads of the web of life? Photograph by Neil Williams.

Glossary

Afforestation / Deforestation

Afforestation is planting trees where there were none before, converting land, usually farmland, to forest. Deforestation is the reverse: removing trees and converting land to another use, for example development, wind farms or open ground.

Agroforestry

Growing systems including both agriculture and forestry in intimate combination. This may be trees with arable (silvo-arable), where the trees are typically in strips with alleys of crops in between; or trees with pasture (silvo-pastoral), where the trees can be spread throughout (eg sheep in an orchard), or laid out in strips with grazing in between. The benefits are a better protected agricultural landscape and potentially higher total productivity.

Ancient Semi-Natural Woods (ASNW)

Any wood that has been in existence since 1600 in England, Wales and Northern Ireland or since 1750 in Scotland. Before this time, tree planting was not common, so it is reckoned that any woodland on the map at that date would have been there for some considerable time and evolved relatively naturally. As such, they tend to include plant and animal communities absent from woods of more recent origin. In these islands almost all woods have been modified in some way by humans, so these ancient woods are only partly 'natural', hence the term Ancient Semi-Natural Woodland.

Ancient trees

Trees of great age and size, often hundreds or even thousands of years old, but also trees that are relatively old or large for their species and in the third and final stage of life. For example, an ancient oak tree might have a girth of three 'hugs', while the short-lived birch would be considered ancient with a girth of just one hug.

Ash dieback

'First confirmed in Britain in 2012, ash dieback, previously known as 'Chalara', is a disease of ash trees caused by a fungus (*Hymenoscyphus fraxineus*). Ash trees across much of England are now symptomatic of ash dieback, and it is expected that the majority of ash trees will subsequently die from or be significantly affected by the disease in the coming years. Currently there is no known efficient prevention or curative treatment.' (FC 2019)

Biodiversity

This is what used to be known as 'nature' or 'wildlife'. It is the vast array of life on Earth, including both different species and genetic diversity within species.

Bio-Energy with Carbon Capture and Storage (BECCS)

This technology does not yet exist! It is the process of growing plants to sequester CO_2, using them to generate bio-energy, then capturing the emitted CO_2 and storing it underground. This 'negative emissions' technology features heavily in some strategies for zero carbon.

Biomass

Here the term refers to woody material used as a fuel. Ideally only wood that cannot find a better use would be included, such as branches, bent stems, low-grade sections and undesirable species of wood. However, as the market has grown, so too have supplies and there is concern that excessive wood is being channelled into biomass to the detriment of forests.

Broadleaf trees

These trees have flat leaves and produce seeds inside fruits. Common broadleaves in UK are oak, ash, beech, maple, birch and alder. They are usually deciduous, but there are also many evergreen broadleaves, such as holm oak, laurel and holly. Their timber is referred to as 'hardwood', as it is usually denser than the 'softwood' of conifers.

Carbon sequestration

The process by which trees and woody plants trap carbon. All plants are carbon-based, but woody plants manage to keep the carbon locked in wood cells. The carbon remains in the wood until the tree dies and decays, or until it is burnt, at which point the carbon is oxidised to CO_2. By making durable items, such as books and houses, out of wood we can continue to sequester the carbon.

Certification

Forest Certification provides an independent check on whether timber has been responsibly produced. In the UK there are two certification schemes: FSC (Forest Stewardship Council) and PEFC (Programme for the Endorsement of

Forest Certification), and they both use the UK Woodland Assurance Standard (UKWAS). You can buy certified products such as paper, wooden implements, boards and timber.

Clearfell

Where a whole stand of trees is felled. This could be anything from a fraction of a hectare to 50 hectares or more. It is a common practice in plantation forestry where the crop is monocultural and even-aged. Though an efficient industrial process for harvesting timber, it leaves little biodiversity above ground and may have detrimental impacts on soils and hydrology.

Climate adaptation

The process by which living beings, both people and plants, adjust to changes in the climate. For example, as the climate warms in the UK, some plants and animals from hotter climes may find it more hospitable here, whilst others will head north to maintain cooler temperatures. Trees also help us adapt to a warmer climate by providing shelter and shade.

Climate breakdown

The terms 'climate change' and 'global warming' do not adequately convey the scale and urgency of changes to our living environment, so the terms 'climate crisis', 'climate chaos' and 'climate breakdown' are often used.

Climate mitigation

Efforts to prevent, reduce or reverse the causes of climate change, namely the emission of greenhouse gases. For example, by reducing the use of fossil fuels, insulating houses, substituting wood for concrete, and sequestering carbon long-term in trees we can slow down the drivers of climate breakdown.

Committee on Climate Change

An independent statutory body established under the Climate Change Act 2008, which advises the UK government on emissions targets and strategies for achieving these and reports on progress towards the targets. It produces well-researched reports, but its advice is not always heeded by government.

Community Interest Company

A type of company introduced by the United Kingdom government in 2005 under the Companies Act 2004, designed for social enterprises that want to use their profits and assets for the public good. CICs are intended to be easy to set up, with all the flexibility and certainty of the company form, but with some special features to ensure they are working for the benefit of the community.

Community Woodland

A community woodland is one partly or completely controlled by the local community through a community woodland group. The woodland may be owned or leased by the group, or managed in partnership with a public or private-sector landowner. Community woodlands are extremely diverse, embracing all woodland types from Ancient Semi-Natural Woods to extensive conifer plantations, and ranging from less than a hectare to over 1,000 hectares in size.

Conifers

Conifers bear cones with seeds, have needle-like or scale-like leaves and are usually evergreen. Common conifers in the UK are Sitka spruce, Norway spruce (Christmas trees), Scots pine, Corsican pine, Leyland cypress, Western Red Cedar and Sequoia. Larch is one of the conifers that loses its needles in winter. The timber they produce is called 'softwood' as it is generally less dense than 'hardwood' from broadleaf trees.

Conservation Area

An area of special architectural or historic interest in which trees (and buildings) have some protection. Trees with a trunk diameter of 75 mm or more at 1.5 m height are protected and it is an offence to prune, fell or damage a tree without first giving notice to the council. The council then has six weeks to consider whether to apply a Tree Preservation Order, or they may discuss alternative works to the tree.

Continuous Cover Forestry (CCF)

An approach to silviculture that aims to maintain a protective forest canopy throughout successive generations of trees. Instead of clearfelling all the mature trees and then restocking the bare site, CCF just fells small groups of trees, or thin strips, or even single trees, then restocks the gaps on a continuous basis. This creates a diverse stand with trees of different ages. It is more complicated, but maintains 'forest conditions' of dappled shade, humidity, the sustaining mycorrhizal network, protection from drying sun and wind, as well as producing woods of great beauty and biodiversity.

Coppice

The practice of repeatedly cutting trees near the base and allowing them to grow up again, producing multiple valuable straight stems. Most broadleaf trees can be coppiced and whole industries have been based on hazel (for thatching spars and fencing), oak (for tanbark) and sweet chestnut (for posts, rails and hop-poles). Coppicing can prolong the life of a tree, with some ash and lime stools being many hundreds of years old.

Cubic metres and tonnes

Timber is usually measured in cubic metres (m^3) or metric tonnes (t). For most UK green wood (freshly felled) one tonne is roughly equivalent to one cubic metre.

Defra

The UK government's Department for Environment, Food & Rural Affairs, responsible for 'safeguarding our natural environment, supporting our world-leading food and farming industry, and sustaining a thriving economy'. The Forestry Commission and Natural England belong to the Defra 'family'.

Ecosystem services

These are the many and varied benefits we get from the natural world around us. There are four broad areas of ecosystem services: provisioning (food, water, timber), regulating (climate, pollination, flooding), supporting (photosynthesis, soil formation, nutrient cycles) and cultural (recreation, education). These services can be quantified and valued.

Forest

The term 'forest' has several meanings. 'The word "forest" is derived from the Latin *foris*, meaning "outside"..."forest" became a term referring to land placed off limits by royal decree...areas where the monarch enjoyed exclusive hunting rights' (Ghazoul). These were the 'wastes' outside the areas of settlement and cultivation, where the nobility hunted deer. 'The word Forest was a legal term – a tract of land within which the Forest Law operated' (Rackham). These hunting 'Forests' may only have been half-wooded. Our modern sense of a forest as an area predominantly covered with trees only emerged in the 19th century with the development of forestry practice in Continental Europe. In the UK, a forest is now defined as 'land under stands of trees with a canopy cover of at least 20 per cent' (UKFS).

Forest bathing

Known in Japan as 'shinrin-yoku', this meditative practice has become popular in Britain. It is a 'nature therapy' and is intended to 'improve immune, cardiovascular and respiratory functioning' (wikipedia). The theory is that a relaxed body 'bathing' the senses in the sounds, smells, sights, tastes and touch of the forest will naturally heal itself.

Forest cover

The area of land covered by trees, obviously. Except it is not quite that simple... Even the most densely packed production forests have rides, streams and occasional glades, so tree cover is often only some 85–90 per cent of the total area. More amenity forests have considerable areas of open ground, and wood pasture could be more than half open ground. Still, according to the UKFS definition, if it is at least 20 per cent covered in trees, it counts as 'forest'. Much of this book is concerned with how and why we lost most of our forest cover and how we might restore it.

Forest gardening

'A forest garden is a designed agronomic system based on trees, shrubs and perennial plants. These are mixed in such a way as to mimic the structure of a natural forest – the most stable and sustainable type of ecosystem in this climate' (Agroforestry Research Trust website). Tall fruit and nut trees are mixed with soft-fruit bushes, herbs and perennial vegetables in a multi-layered forest.

FSC

The Forest Stewardship Council (FSC) operates an international certification standard that has ten principles covering legal issues and use rights, community relations and workers' rights, environmental impacts and conservation, forest management and monitoring. These have been filtered through the particular requirements of UK forestry to produce our local UK Woodland Assurance Standard (UKWAS).

Holocene

Our current geological epoch, which started about 12,000 years ago, following the last Ice

Age. A warmer and more stable climate enabled the development of human agriculture and civilisations. Before this period, humans mostly lived hunter-gatherer lifestyles.

Hunter-gatherer societies

These were/are societies foraging food from wild plants and hunting wild animals, as opposed to agricultural societies which gain food from domesticated plants and animals. About 90 per cent of human history was spent as hunter-gatherers, through the Palaeolithic and Mesolithic periods, ending for most societies around 10,000 years ago with the dawn of the Neolithic Revolution.

Independent Panel on Forestry

Set up in 2011 following the debacle over the attempted sell-off of the public forest estate (FC woods). They gathered evidence and reported in 2012 with advice to government on woodland policy, a re-evaluation of our public woods and ideas on developing a new 'wood culture'.

Monoculture

A forest with only one predominant species. Many plantations are established as monocultures, for example Sitka spruce, in order to maximise returns by streamlining the industrial production process. Identical trees planted in lines at regular spacing yield a consistent product in the least time. Monocultures lack diversity, clearly, and are seen by the public as monotonous and by wildlife groups as lacking in biodiversity. They are also vulnerable to devastation by disease, as illustrated by the fate of larch from *Phytophthora ramorum*. The alternative is mixed woodland.

Mycorrhiza

Literally 'fungus root', this is a symbiotic association between a fungus and a tree. The fungus grows either within the root or on its surface and provides the root with a more efficient interface with the soil for water and nutrients. In return, the tree provides the fungus with sugars, which it cannot produce itself.

Native / non-native

The 'native flora' of the British Isles was determined around 6,000 BCE when these islands were cut off from Continental Europe by rising sea levels. The theory is that, after the previous Ice Age, plants and animals migrated back northwards under natural conditions until the sea barrier prevented any further colonisation. At that point the drawbridge was raised and anything that got here in time is considered our 'native flora' (and fauna) and anything that did not make the cut is considered 'exotic' or 'alien'. Our natural habitats have evolved since then with these ingredients (and our interventions) to produce our characteristic plant and animal communities, and these native trees consequently support greater biodiversity. Trees can also be native to certain areas within Britain but not others, such as Scots pine in Scotland and beech in southern England. However, several factors undermine this exclusive situation: clearly, given more time, more plants would have got here if not for the English Channel, so we could have a richer north European flora suited to these climes; with a changing climate, the plants that are here may not be best suited in the long term; plant and animal imports over centuries and recent global trade have already massively changed our domestic populations (think rhododendron or grey squirrel); pollen and fungal spores can blow in on the wind from the Continent, affecting the genetics and health of our native trees.

Natural capital

Formerly known as 'the natural world', then as 'natural resources', now repackaged as 'natural capital'. The idea is that the world's rocks, soils, plants and animals are seen as capital stocks, from which flow a steady income of 'ecosystem services'. That's one way of looking at it – one that informs much of government thinking.

Natural regeneration

Trees setting seed and growing a new generation of seedling trees. It is one way of restocking felled stands and of establishing trees on bare ground, the alternative being planting. Often restocking uses both planting and natural regeneration.

Panelboards

Medium-density fibreboard (MDF) is made from wood fibres with binder under high pressure and temperature. Oriented strand board (OSB) is made of strands or flakes of wood oriented lengthways in layers and bound by adhesives; it is also known as 'Stirling Board' after the factory location in

Scotland. Particleboard is made of woodchips bound and pressed together. It is often faced with melamine for worktops.

Plantations on Ancient Woodland Sites (PAWS)

Many ancient woods have undergone some sort of alteration, for example in the 1960s and 1970s many were felled and replanted with fast-growing exotic conifers, such as Norway spruce, Japanese larch, Douglas fir and Western hemlock. Others were planted with uniform crops of beech, others with mixtures of spruce and oak. The resulting woods are termed PAWS and it is an urgent ambition of conservationists to restore these woods to native tree cover.

Pollard

A tree that has been repeatedly cut at about head height, its stems harvested for poles or animal fodder. Pollards are particularly useful where there are grazing animals, as the regrowth is beyond browse height. They are often seen in wood pasture, where trees can reach great size and age.

Productive woodland

Woods and forests that prioritise timber production, as opposed to wildlife, landscape or recreation. All the conifer plantations of the post-war era were intended as productive woodland, and most have achieved this. Hardwood/broadleaf woods can also be 'productive' and yield good crops of oak.

Resilience

The ability to withstand and recover from shocks. This is an increasing concern in the face of climate breakdown. A forest's resilience is a function of diversity of tree and other forest species, genetic diversity within each tree species, functioning forest soils and the structural diversity of the stands.

Restock

After felling, the resulting open areas are restocked with new trees. This can be by planting, coppice regrowth, natural regeneration, or a combination of these.

Restructure

There are many post-war plantations that are even-aged monocultures of exotic conifers with low biodiversity value. There is an opportunity to restructure these stands when they end their rotation. This means aiming for a greater number of smaller stands of trees, leading to greater structural diversity across the forest; more diversity of species within each stand, both conifer and broadleaf; restoring natural features such as streams, ponds, bogs, heathland, ride edges and native woodland.

Rewilding

'Rewilding is the large-scale restoration of ecosystems where nature can take care of itself, enabling natural processes to shape land and sea, repair damaged ecosystems and restore degraded landscapes' (Rewilding Britain).

Riparian woodland

Woods that stretch along the banks of rivers and streams, creating an edge habitat of great benefit to the aquatic ecosystem. They also protect water courses from pollution by fertiliser, pesticide and soil run-off.

Rotation

In classical silviculture, trees are planted, grown till they reach the desired size, then harvested like a crop. This length of time is the rotation, the idea being that you then start again and repeat on a cycle forever. Conifers are quick-growing and their rotations can be around 40 years or even shorter. Oaks might have a rotation of over 100 years.

Semi-natural habitat

All the natural habitats of the UK have been modified over the centuries, so 'semi-natural' is the best we can hope for. Nevertheless, these habitats have ecological communities of great diversity and value, such as chalk grassland, heathland, fen.

Site of Special Scientific Interest (SSSI)

A formal conservation designation of special interest to science, either geological or biological. SSSI sites are administered by Natural England, Natural Resources Wales, Scottish Natural Heritage and Northern Ireland Environment Agency. They cover important habitats such as some ancient woods, grassland and heathland.

Sustainable Forest Management

In theory this is management that could continue forever without depleting the forest. The UK Forest Standard describes the elements of sustainable forest management, including consideration of biodiversity, climate change, the historic environment, landscape, people, soil, water and general forestry practice.

Thinning

The periodic removal of some trees from a stand to make room for the others to grow and yield a modest return in the meantime. Much has been written about the science of thinning – when to thin, how much to cut, which trees to take. It is an opportunity for the forester to shape a stand of trees for the desired outcomes. In very windy upland stands, thinning is not possible because it exposes the remaining trees to windblow and the collapse of the stand.

Tree Preservation Order (TPO)

TPOs can apply to single trees, or groups or woodlands and they protect trees from felling, pruning and damage. These works require permission from the local authority and consent can be subject to conditions.

UK Forestry Standard

UKFS was first launched in 1998 and sets out the government's approach to sustainable forest management. This underpins acceptable forestry practice and it is necessary to comply in order to receive Forestry Commission grants.

Veteran trees

Trees with a history. Like a war veteran, they may be young or old but they bear the marks of experience; for example a lost limb, large dead branches or a hollow trunk. These features will grow in ecological interest as the tree ages.

Wildwood

This is the imagined woodland vegetation covering these islands before human intervention, pieced together using pollen records. Oliver Rackham has identified a number of 'wildwood provinces' around 4500 BCE, with southeast England dominated by lime, southwest England, Wales, northern England and southern Scotland favouring oak and hazel, pine in the Scottish Highlands and birch in the far north.

Wood culture

This describes a way of life intimately integrated with trees and woods, where these are meaningful in our lives. We have obviously lost this culture, along with most of our woods. In this book we show how trees are as important as ever and how we can develop a more sustainable culture with more trees.

Wood meadow

This is similar to Wood Pasture, except that the open areas are mown instead of grazed by animals. Wood meadows have a savanna-like appearance and can support a great diversity of flora. Once common in Europe during Medieval times, they have only survived around the Baltic Sea.

Wood pasture

Wood pasture is usually a mosaic of woodland, scrubby thickets, open grassland, ancient trees and grazing animals. This diversity of habitat supports a rich community of flora and fauna, constantly evolving and changing under pressure from browsing and trampling. Wood pasture make a very pleasing landscape, something like a temperate 'savanna'.

Woodland Social Enterprise (WSE)

WSEs operate within woodland settings to deliver primarily social benefits (and sometimes environmental benefits) from selling goods and services; they then reinvest their profits back into the local community. The distinguishing feature of a Woodland Social Enterprise, as opposed to a volunteer group, is that it trades commercially. It could be selling wood products such as logs and timber or services such as education and health provision, or using the wood as a venue for events, courses, recreation, woodland burials or weddings. The WSE operators could also be marketing their own expertise as consultants.

Further Reading

General Reading

Abram, D. (1997) *The Spell of the Sensuous*, Vintage

Auden, W. H. (1952–3) *Bucolics*: 'Woods', reissued in *Collected Poems* (2004), Faber & Faber

Barnes, G. & Williamson, T. (2015) *Rethinking Ancient Woodland: the archaeology and history of woods in Norfolk*, University of Hertfordshire Press

Baker, J. A. (1969) *The Hill of Summer*, Collins

Berners-Lee, M. (2019) *There Is No Planet B – A Handbook for the Make or Break Years*, Cambridge University Press

Bryant, W. Logan (2019) *Sprout Lands: Tending the Endless Gift of Trees*, W. W. Norton & Company

Capra, F. & Luisi, P. L. (2014) *The Systems View of Life: A Unifying Vision*, Cambridge University Press

Clare, John (1820) *Poems descriptive of rural life and scenery*, Taylor and Hessey

Clifford, S. and King, A. (2006) *England in Particular*, Hodder & Stoughton Ltd

Common Ground (2008) *Community Orchards Handbook*, Green Books

Common Ground (1990) *Trees be Company: An Anthology of Poetry*, Green Books

Cooper, A. (Ed.) (2016) *Arboreal*, Little Toller Books

Deakin, R. (2007) *Wildwood: A Journey Through Trees*, Penguin

Edwards, I., (Ed.) (2010) *Woodlanders: New Life in Britain's Forests*, Saraband

Farjon, A. (2017) *Ancient Oaks: In the English landscape*, Kew Publishing

Fiennes, P. (2017) *Oak and Ash and Thorn – The ancient woods and new forests of Britain*, Oneworld

Foot, D. (2010) *Woods & People*, The History Press

Griffiths, J. (2008) *Wild: An Elemental Journey*, Penguin

Hardy, T. (1886–87) *The Woodlanders*, Macmillan

Hardman, I. (2020) *The Natural Health Service: What the Great Outdoors can do for your mind*, Atlantic Books

Harrison, R. Pogue (1993) *Forests: The Shadow of Civilisation*, University of Chicago Press

Haskell, D. G. (2012) *The Forest Unseen – A Year's Watch in Nature*, Penguin

Haskell, D. G. (2017) *The Songs of Trees – Stories from nature's Great Connectors*, Viking

Helm, D. (2019) *Green and Prosperous Land – A Blueprint for Rescuing the British Countryside*, William Collins

Hemery, G. (2020) *Tall Trees Short Stories*, Wood Wide Works

Hemery, G. & Simblet, S. (2014) *The New Sylva*, Bloomsbury

Hopkins, G. M. (2019) 'Binsey Poplars' from *Gerard Manley Hopkins: Poems and Prose*, Penguin

Johnson, R. (republished in 2011) *The Book of the Green Man*, Unifrom Books

Juniper, T. (2015) *What Nature Does for Britain*, Profile Books

Kunial, Z. (2019) *Us*, Faber & Faber

Lent, J. (2017) *The Patterning Instinct: A Cultural History of Humanity's Search for Meaning*, Prometheus Books

Louv, R. (2005) *Last Child in the Woods*, Algonquin Books of Chapel Hill

Lloyd, C. (2008) *What On Earth Happened?* Bloomsbury

Lyon, N. (2016) *Uprooted: On the trail of the Green Man*, Faber & Faber

Mabey, R. (2008) *Beechcombings, The Narrative of Trees*, Vintage

Mew, C. 'The Trees are Down', from *The Rambling Sailor* (1929), Poetry Bookshop

Monbiot, G. (2014) *Feral*, Penguin

Monbiot, G. (2017) *Out Of The Wreckage*, Verso

Oswald, A. (2005), *Woods etc*, Faber & Faber

Peterken, G. (1996) *Natural Woodland*, Cambridge University Press

Powers, R. (2018) *The Overstory*, Vintage

Rackham, O. (1990) *Trees and Woodlands in the British Landscape*, Dent & Sons Ltd, 2nd ed

Rackham, O. (2010) *Woodlands*, Collins

Rackham, O. (2014) *The Ash Tree*, Little Toller Books

Raskin, B. & Osborn, S. (Eds.) (2019) *The Agroforestry Handbook: Agroforestry for the UK*, Soil Association Ltd

Raworth, K. (2017) *Doughnut Economics*, Random House

Sinden, N. for Common Ground (1989) *In A Nutshell*, Common Ground

Smith, J. and Thompson, L. (Ed.) for Common Ground (2016) *Tree Tales: A Celebration of Exeter's Trees*, Little Toller Books

Snyder, G. (1990) *The Practice of the Wild*, North Point Press

MacLean, S. (1952) 'Hallaig' (trans. by Seamus Heaney), *Hallaig and Other Poems: Selected Poems of Sorley MacLean*, Polygon

Stafford, F. (2017) *The Long, Long Life of Trees*, Harvard University Press

Tree, I. (2018) *Wilding*, Picador

Tudge, C. (2006) *The Secret Life of Trees*, Penguin Books

Williamson, T., Barnes, G., Pillatt, T. (2017) *Trees in England: Management and disease since 1600*, University of Hertfordshire Press

Wohlleben, P. (2017) *The Hidden Life of Trees*, William Collins

Wohlleben, P. (2018) *The Secret Network of Nature*, The Bodley Head

State of Nature

Centre for Alternative Technology (2019) *Zero Carbon Britain: Rising to the climate emergency*

Committee on Climate Change (2018) *Land Use: Reducing emissions and preparing for climate change*

Committee on Climate Change (2019) *Net Zero: The UK's contribution to stopping global warming*

Committee on Climate Change (2020) *Land Use: Policies for a net zero UK*

Confor (2017) *A Common Countryside Policy: Securing a prosperous green future after Brexit*

Defra (2018) *A Green Future: Our 25 year plan to improve the environment*

Forestry Commission (2017) *Public Opinion of Forestry*

Forestry Climate Change Working Group (2018) *Action Plan for Climate Change Adaptation of Forests, Woods and Trees in England*

Harwatt, H. & Hayek, M. (2019) *Eating Away at Climate Change with Negative Emissions – Repurposing UK agricultural land to meet climate goals*, Harvard Law School

Hayhow, D., et al. (2019) *State of Nature 2019*, The State of Nature partnership

Independent Panel on Forestry (2012) *Final Report*, Defra

Lawton, J., et al. (2010) *Making Space for Nature: A review of England's wildlife sites and ecological network*, Report to Defra

Packham, C. (2018) *A Peoples' Manifesto for Wildlife: Draft one*, Chris Packham et al.

Read, D. et al. (eds.) (2009) *Combating climate change – a role for UK forests*, The Stationery Office

Woodland Trust (2011) *The State of the UK's Forests, Woods and Trees*

Woodland Trust (2015) *The Economic Benefits of Woodland*

WWF (2020) *Living Planet Report 2020: Bending the curve of biodiversity loss*. Almond, R. E. A., Grooten M. and Petersen, T. (Eds). WWF, Gland, Switzerland

Restoration and Sustainable Forestry

Forestry Commission (2017) *The UK Forestry Standard*

Harmer, R., Kerr, G., Thompson, R. (2010) *Managing Native Broadleaved Woodland*, The Stationery Office

Peterken, G. (2002) *Reversing the Habitat Fragmentation of British Woodlands*, WWF

Pryor, S., Curtis, T., Peterken, G. (2002) *Restoring Plantations on Ancient Woodland Sites*, Woodland Trust

Spencer, J. (2018/19) 'Forest Resilience in British Forests, Woods & Plantations – Articles 1 to 4, in *Quarterly Journal of Forestry*, 112/1 (Jan 2018) to 113/3 (July 2019)

Thompson, R., Humphrey, J., Harmer, R., Ferris, R. (2003) *Restoration of Native Woodland on Ancient Woodland Sites*, Forestry Commission

Woodland Trust (2005) *The Conservation and Restoration of Plantation on Ancient Woodland Sites*

The Wildlife Trusts (2010) *A Living Landscape*

Trees in the Landscape

CPRE (2011) *A Little Rough Guide Around the Hedges*

Devon Hedge Group (2014) *Wood Fuel from Hedges*, Devon County Council

Forestry Commission (2016) *Woodland Land Cover by County*

Peterken, G. (2015) 'Woodland History in the British Isles – An Interaction of Environmental and Cultural Forces' in *Europe's Changing Woods and Forests*, Ed. Kirby & Watkins, CABI

Newton, A. et al. (2019) *Trends in Natural Capital, Ecosystem Services and Economic Development in Dorset*, Bournemouth University

Woodland Trust (2012) *Trees Outside Woods*

The Urban Forest

Britt, C. & Johnston, M. (2008) *Trees in Towns II*, HMSO

Forestry Commission (2010) *The Case for Trees in Development and the Urban Environment*

Hammond, A., Hassall, J., Harrison, C. (2017) *Making London's Woodlands Work*, Lantern (UK) Ltd & Forestry Commission

Rogers, K., Jarratt, T., Hansford, D. (2011) *Torbay's Urban Forest Assessing Urban Forest Effects and Values*, Treeconomics

Rogers, K., Sacre, K., Goodenough, J., Doick, K. (2015) *Valuing London's Urban Forest*, Treeconomics

Urban Forestry and Woodlands Advisory Committee (2015) *Our Vision for a Resilient Urban Forest*, Urban FWAC Network

Community Engagement

Dandy, N. (2018) 'Woodland Social Enterprise Innovation and Resilience in the Forest Sector', *Quarterly Journal of Forestry* (July 2018)

Lawrence, A., & Ambrose-Oji, B. (2013) *A Framework for Sharing Experiences of Community Woodland Groups*, Forestry Commission

Swade, K., Walker, A., Walton, M., Barker, K. (2013) *Community Management of Local Authority Woodlands in England*, Shared Assets

Woodland Trust (2011) *Community Ownership for Woodland Management and Creation*

Health and Wellbeing

Archard, J., Taragon, S., Saunders, G., Pasteur, K. (2018) 'A Magnet For Those Who Need It: Woodland Social Enterprises and work with in-need groups' *Ecos* 39 (6)

National Tree Safety Group (2011) *Common Sense Risk Management of Trees*, Forestry Commission

O'Brien, L. (2006) 'Strengthening Heart and Mind: Using woodlands to improve mental and physical wellbeing', *Unasylva Forests and Human Health*, 57/224 (2006/2), FAO

Woodland Trust (2017) *Space for People: Targeting action for woodland access*

Shackell, A. and Walter, R. (2012) *Greenspace design for health and wellbeing*, Forestry Commission

Design and Make

Carruthers, A. (1994) *Edward Barnsley and his Workshop: Arts and Crafts in the Twentieth Century*, White Cockade Publishing

Fung, S. (2016) *Architecture by Hand: Inspired by nature*, Clearview

Gunnell, K., Murphy, B., Williams, C. (2013) *Designing for Biodiversity: A technical guide for new and existing buildings*, RIBA Publishing

Harris, R. (1993) *Discovering Timber-Framed Buildings*, Shire Publications

Law, B. (2010) *The Woodland House*, Permanent Publications

Makepeace, J. et al (2017) *Beyond Parnham*, John Makepeace

Mols, S. (1999) *Wooden Furniture in Herculaneum: form, technique and function*, Brill Academic Publishers

Reynolds, A. (2010) *Timber for building: turning trees into houses*, Low Impact Living Initiative

Sturt, G. (1923) *The Wheelwright Shop*, CUP

Wilson, P. (2017) *The Modern Timber House in the UK – New paradigms and technologies*, Arcamedia Ltd

Watson, J. (2019) *Lo-TEK Design by Radical Indigenism*, Taschen

Farming with Trees

Confor (2017) *Farm Forestry*

Crawford, M. (2010) *Creating A Forest Garden*, Green Books

Defra (2018) *The Future Farming and Environment Evidence Compendium*

Defra (2011) *The Natural Choice: Securing the value of nature*

Defra (2019) *Agriculture in the United Kingdom 2018*

Hart, R. (1991) *The Forest Garden*, The Institute for Social Inventions

RSA Food, Farming & Countryside Commission (2019) *Our Future in the Land*, RSA

Smith, J. and Westaway, S. (2020) *Wakelyns Agroforestry: Resilience through diversity*, Organic Research Centre

Wolfe, M. (2001) *Functional Biodiversity*, Elm Farm Research Centre

Future Forests

Browning, G. (2019) 'Rewilding, the view from a Wilder Lake District Valley', *Quarterly Journal of Forestry*, 113/2 (Apr 2019)

Cairngorms National Park Authority (2018) *Cairngorms National Park Forest Strategy 2018*

Charter for Trees, Woods and People (2017)

Defra (2017) *Forestry in England: Seeing the wood for the trees*, Department Environment, Food and Rural Affairs Committee

Friends of the Earth (2019) *Finding the Land to Double Tree Cover*

Jannaway, K. (1991) *Abundant Living in the Coming Age of the Tree*, Movement for Compassionate Living

Larsen, J. B. (2012) 'Close-to-Nature Forest management: The Danish approach to Sustainable Forestry', in Garcia, J. M. and Casero, J. J. D. (Eds.) *Sustainable Forest Management – Current research*, InTech open science, 2012, 119–218

Rewilding Britain (2019) *Rewilding and Climate Breakdown: How restoring nature can help decarbonise the UK*

Vera, Frans (2000) *Grazing Ecology and Forest History*, CABI Publishing

Woodland Trust (2017) *Putting Down New Roots: Essays on woods, trees and the landscape of the future*

Woodland Trust (2018) *Sustainable Land Management: Putting trees and woods at the heart of a new sustainable land management policy*

Woodland Trust (2020) *Emergency Tree Plan for the UK: How to increase tree cover and address the nature and climate emergency*

Useful Resources

AGROFORESTRY IN EUROPE
agforward.eu
Useful research and information network for agroforestry in Europe.

ANCIENT TREE FORUM
ancienttreeforum.co.uk
Raising awareness of the value of old trees and lobbying for their protection.

ARCHITECTURAL ASSOCIATION AT HOOKE PARK
hookepark.aaschool.ac.uk
A 150-hectare working forest in Dorset owned and operated by the AA with a growing educational facility for design, workshop and construction.

BIOFUELWATCH
biofuelwatch.org.uk
Information, advocacy and campaigning in relation to the climate, environmental, human-rights and public-health impacts of large-scale industrial bio-energy.

CAMPAIGN TO PROTECT RURAL ENGLAND
cpre.org.uk
Campaigning for a countryside that's rich in nature, accessible to everyone and responding to the climate emergency.

CENTRE FOR ALTERNATIVE TECHNOLOGY
cat.org.uk
Educational charity dedicated to researching and communicating solutions for environmental change.

COMMITTEE ON CLIMATE CHANGE
theccc.org.uk
Providing independent advice to government on building a low-carbon economy and preparing for climate change.

COMMON GROUND
commonground.org.uk
A small, grassroots organisation that collaborates openly to reconnect people with nature and inspires communities to become responsible for their local environment.

COMMUNITY WOOD RECYCLING
communitywoodrecycling.org.uk
A nationwide network of wood-recycling social enterprises.

COMMUNITY WOODLANDS (WALES)
llaisygoedwig.org.uk
A grassroots membership network that aims to represent and support community woodland groups and practitioners across Wales.

COMMUNITY WOODLANDS (ENGLAND)
communitywoodland.org
Woodland Trust help and advice for starting and running a community woodland.

COMMUNITY WOODLANDS ASSOCIATION (SCOTLAND)
communitywoods.org
Promoting and supporting Scotland's community woodlands.

CONFOR
confor.org.uk
A membership organisation for sustainable forestry and wood-using businesses.

FORESTRY COMMISSION
forestry.gov.uk
 TREE DISEASES
 forestry.gov.uk/treediseases
 TREE PESTS
 forestry.gov.uk/treepests

FOREST RESEARCH
forestresearch.gov.uk
Britain's principal organisation for forestry and tree-related research in support of sustainable forestry.

FOREST SCHOOL ASSOCIATION
forestschoolassociation.org
Promoting and supporting best practice, cohesion and quality of Forest Schools across the UK.

FOREST STEWARDSHIP COUNCIL (FSC)
fsc-uk.org/en-uk
International, non-governmental organisation dedicated to promoting responsible management of the world's forests.

FRIENDS OF THE EARTH
friendsoftheearth.uk/trees
A petition to double tree cover across the UK.

GROWN IN BRITAIN
growninbritain.org
Developing a new 'wood culture' by engaging and changing attitudes and practices to ensure the future success of the UK's woods and forests.

HEDGELINK
hedgelink.org.uk
Supporting people and organisations with information, knowledge and ideas about hedges.

IPCC
www.ipcc.ch
The Intergovernmental Panel on Climate Change (IPCC) is the United Nations body for assessing the science related to climate change.

MAKING LOCAL WOODS WORK
makinglocalwoodswork.org
A partnership working to support and grow Woodland Social Enterprises around the UK.

NATIONAL FOREST
nationalforest.org
An ambitious and imaginative project to establish the first forest at scale in England for over 1,000 years.

NATIONAL FOREST INVENTORY
forestry.gov.uk/inventory
A programme monitoring woods and trees in Great Britain.

NATIONAL TREE SAFETY GROUP
ntsgroup.org.uk
A number of organisations with an interest in tree-risk management, shaping national approaches.

NATURAL RESOURCES WALES
naturalresources.wales
Welsh Government-sponsored body ensuring that the natural resources of Wales are sustainably maintained.

NHS FOREST
nhsforest.org
Improving the health and wellbeing of patients, staff and communities by increasing access to green space on or near NHS land.

NORTHERN IRELAND FOREST SERVICE
daera-ni.gov.uk/topics/forestry
Executive agency of Defra entrusted with the development of forestry in Northern Ireland.

THE ORCHARD PROJECT
theorchardproject.org.uk
National charity dedicated to the creation, restoration and celebration of community orchards.

ORGANIC RESEARCH CENTRE
organicresearchcentre.com
Independent research centre for the development of organic/agroecological food production and land management.

PROGRAMME FOR THE ENDORSEMENT OF FOREST CERTIFICATION
pefc.org
Endorsing certification to promote the sustainable management of forests.

REWILDING BRITAIN
rewildingbritain.org.uk
Champion of rewilding in Britain and acting as a catalyst for debate and action to tackle the climate emergency and the extinction crisis.

ROYAL FORESTRY SOCIETY
rfs.org.uk
Largest and longest-established education charity promoting the wise management of woods in England, Wales and Northern Ireland.

SCOTTISH FORESTRY
forestry.gov.scot
Scottish Government agency responsible for forestry policy, support, regulations and planting targets.

SMALL WOODS ASSOCIATION
smallwoods.org.uk
National organisation (in England) for woodland owners, workers and supporters.

SOIL ASSOCIATION
soilassociation.org
Membership charity campaigning for healthy, humane and sustainable food, farming and land use. Provides certification services for FSC and PECF Forest Management and Chain of Custody worldwide.

SYLVA FOUNDATION
sylva.org.uk
An environmental charity helping trees and people grow together. Focused on science, education, forestry and wood.

TREE COUNCIL
treecouncil.org.uk
A charity that provides information, organises events and supports trees and hedges in the community, particularly through its 'tree warden' scheme.

TREES FOR CITIES
treesforcities.org
A UK charity working at home and internationally to improve lives by planting trees in cities.

TREE ECOSYSTEM SERVICES
treeconomics.co.uk
A social enterprise working to highlight the value of trees, working with community groups, research organisations, public bodies, municipalities and private business.

TREES FOR LIFE
treesforlife.org.uk
A pioneering conservation charity aiming to revitalise wild forest in the Scottish Highlands, providing space for wildlife to flourish and communities to thrive.

TREERESPONSIBILITY
treesponsibility.com
Focuses on tree planting for flood mitigation in Calderdale, West Yorkshire.

TRILLION TREES
trilliontrees.org
A joint venture between Birdlife International, Wildlife Conservation Society and WWF to inspire people to protect and restore one trillion trees by 2050.

UKWAS
ukwas.org.uk
The UK Woodland Assurance Standard (UKWAS) is an independent certification standard for verifying sustainable woodland management in the UK.

WAKELYNS
wakelyns.co.uk
An organic rotation agroforestry farm in Suffolk, one of the longest-established and most diverse agroforestry sites in the UK.

THE WILD NETWORK
thewildnetwork.com
Aiming to 'rewild childhood' by overcoming the barriers of fear of danger, lack of time, shrinking space and the dominance of tech.

THE WILDLIFE TRUSTS
wildlifetrusts.org
The Wildlife Trusts is comprised of the 46 individual Wildlife Trusts in the UK and offers a stong voice for the collective movement.

WOODLAND TRUST
woodlandtrust.org.uk
The largest tree and wood conservation charity in the UK. Advocating tree planting, restoration of damaged ancient woods, protection of woods and trees. They also manage over 1,000 woods open to the public.

Index

Acknowledgements

For their help in developing the text, many thanks to Dave Dixon, Karen Wimhurst, Tim Holt-Wilson, Angela King, Adrian Newton, Daniel Keech and Neil Sinden.

For their many helpful contributions and support, many thanks to Richard Mabey, Judi Dench, Martin Stanley, George Peterken, Jos Smith, Keith Kirby, Jonathan Spencer, Sheila Ward (Forest Research Statistics), Ed Bersey, Mark Broadmeadow (FC), Guy Shrubsole (FOE), Ceris Jones (NFU), Adam Dutton (ONS), Sue Clifford, Donald McPhillimy (Reforesting Scotland), Kenton Rogers (Treeconomics), Rob Allen (Citu), Eleanor Harris (Confor), Ian Tubby (Forestry Commission), Gary Fuller (King's College London), Andrew Painting (Mar Lodge Estate), Gareth Browning (FC Ennerdale), Barry Freeman (Tree Warden), Matt Taylor, Helen Browning (Soil Association), Dave Rickwood (Woodland Trust), David Wolfe (Wakelyns), Andy Howard (Doddington), Jo Smith (Organic Research Centre).

R. W.
Shaftesbury, Dorset, 2020
livingwithtrees.co.uk

Opposite: *Tree of Life* by Romy Blümel

Little Toller Books
FORD, PINEAPPLE LANE, DORSET
w. littletoller.co.uk   e. books@littletoller.co.uk